SONG LEADING

Dean B. McIntyre

DISCIPLESHIP RESOURCES
MATERIALS FOR GROWTH IN CHRISTIAN FAITH AND LIFE
P.O. Box 189 • Nashville, TN 37202 • Phone (615) 340-7285

Library of Congress Catalog Card No.: 89-51043

ISBN 0-88177-079-5

DR079B

Contents

Foreword

Song Leading is addressed to the persons in the local church who have the responsibility for the ministry of music within the context of worship. Dean McIntyre offers encouragement and ideas for those volunteer music directors and choir members who have little or no professional training and who desire to try alternatives that demand neither extensive financial obligations nor full-time commitment.

It is also for all those who have responsibility for leading worship, with special emphasis on the pastor, choir, music director, and accompanist, offering scores of specific suggestions. The key objective of this excellent resource is to strengthen and promote congregational worship through song by giving direction to the worship leaders.

This book fills a gap, as few resources exist for volunteers in the ministry of music serving churches of small and medium membership whose budget for music is limited.

Leading the people of God in worship is a responsibility that requires continual self-reflection, evaluation, and spiritual and musical growth. This book speaks to those who are convinced that all persons who participate in church music can find new opportunities to expand their service to God and to the congregation.

DIANA SANCHEZ
Director, Church Music Resources
General Board of Discipleship
The United Methodist Church

Introduction

For twenty centuries, whenever Christians have gathered to worship and praise their Lord, there has been music. Both Old and New Testaments are filled with passages that speak of music in worship. The twenty-sixth chapter of Matthew tells us that in the Upper Room, as Jesus and the disciples celebrated the Passover and instituted the celebration of the Lord's Supper, they concluded their meal with the singing of a hymn. Even one entire book in the Old Testament (the Psalms) consists of the lyrics of some of the earliest and longest lasting songs of the Jewish and Christian churches.

Ancient Hebrew temple worship cultivated a great tradition of formal music making. The Jews considered it to be such an important element that they assigned the responsibility for worship music to a group of professional worship leaders, the Levites.

A wonderful picture is painted in the early chapters of 2 Chronicles of Solomon building and dedicating the temple. It describes the thousands of laborers and overseers, the precious metals used, the beams, posts, and carvings, the altar, the courts, the lamps, and the flowers. Chapter 5 describes the dedication of the completed temple and the Levites bringing the Ark of the Covenant and the Tabernacle into the most holy place of the temple "under the wings of the cherubims." Verse 12 tells of the musicians being arrayed in their white linen, their cymbals, psalteries, and harps and of the 120 priestly trumpet players. Verses 13 and 14 conclude with a description of what happened as they concluded the dedication of the temple. That description serves as an aim of all church musicians and worship leaders even today in Christian worship: "It came to pass, as the singers and instrumentalists were as one, making one sound of praise and thanksgiving to the Lord; and when they lifted up their voice with the trumpets and cymbals and instruments of music and praised the Lord . . . then the house was filled with a cloud, even the house of the Lord, so that the priests could not stand to minister by reason of the cloud; for the glory of the Lord had filled the house of God." The message is clear. When the singers and instrumentalists had prepared their hearts, committed their talents, and offered their music in worship of God, God was so pleased that the temple was filled with the majesty of the divine presence so that even the priests could not carry out their priestly duties.

It is not difficult to see the relationship between the modern Christian church choir—for children, youth, and adults—and those Levite priests. Today, just as centuries earlier, we encourage persons to commit themselves to God and church by giving time and talent in the preparation of hymns, psalms, and spiritual songs to lead the congregation in worship. We physically separate them out of the congregation by placing the choir in a "loft" or other choir area; we stage a processional and a recessional to mark the beginning and end of the formal worship hour; we spend hundreds and thousands of dollars on music to sing and instruments to accompany that singing; we even drape our choirs in fine, costly robes with stoles to symbolize their priestly function as worship leaders. All this is evidence of the importance we attribute to the role of music in our worship.

Most of our churches, however, are removed from the glories of Jewish temple worship by centuries of history and tradition, by generations of theological diversity, and certainly by differences of financial resources. But the similarity of purpose remains. We should still strive to bring the singers and instrumentalists together as one in worship so that God's presence is revealed as an immediate and powerful force.

In the villages of Israel, far removed from the practice of temple worship in Jerusalem, a different tradition of music and worship was cultivated in the synagogues. It was led by cantors, singers who had probably been trained in the practice of temple worship and had been Levites themselves. They led synagogue worship as soloist and leader of congregational singing.

The synagogue music and worship tradition became the model for the early Christian church and remains so today. In addition to the somewhat Levitical nature of many of our church choral programs, we all seek to encourage and develop strong and vital congregational singing. We may still place the leadership responsibilities for worship and music leadership in the hands and voices of trained professionals, but the task of those professionals is now to enable and lead the people in participating together in worship and music. Worship has become a participatory event rather than a spectator event. Worship is something all of us do rather than something that is done by a few for the rest of us.

Throughout the post-Reformation era, congregational singing spread. The early American seekers of religious freedom—the English, Germans, French, and Dutch who settled the colonies—all brought their song books and Psalters with them. Through the revivals and camp meetings of the eighteenth and nineteenth centuries, congregational singing took on an even more prominent role in worship. The work of Isaac Watts, Charles Wesley, Fanny Crosby, and others resulted in thousands of hymns covering a broad range of theology and style.

The great Danish theologian Søren Kierkegäard compared worship to drama. He thought of the congregation—the people in the pews—as the actors. He thought of the worship leaders—pastor, musicians, and lay participants—as assistants, or perhaps the stage crew. If the congregation and worship leaders are the actors and assistants, then who is the audience? Kierkegaard says it is God.

God watches the drama unfold in churches of all sizes and theological persuasions every time the actors gather. It is to God that the actors deliver their lines in the form of hymns, songs, prayers, liturgy, sacrament, and sermon. God is our audience.

In the drama of Sunday worship, with cast, crew, and audience assembled, what is the role of music? How can music best be used to enable the principal actors, the supporting cast, and the crew to play their parts? Later chapters will deal in detail with these questions as they relate specifically to congregation, choir, pastor, director, and accompanist, but for now, consider them in a more general sense.

When we gather for worship on Sunday morning, what do we want to do? Certainly we want to offer our praise and thanksgiving to God. But there are other aims of worship. Worship should proclaim the good news of salvation and God's grace. Worship should teach and instruct in the tenets of our faith. Worship must be sensitive to the spiritual and emotional condition of its participants and seek to minister to the varied needs of the worshipers. In these four aspects of worship—praise, proclamation, education, and ministry—we discover the role of music.

Music and Praise

It is Easter Sunday. As the worshipers arrive, all are aware that this is not just another Sunday morning. They have struggled with their own sinfulness and the call to repentance during the weeks of Lent. The somber tones of the hymns and sermons have established a subdued, introspective mood. The Maundy Thursday and Good Friday services brought to mind the suffering, death, and burial of the Savior of the World. But now it is Sunday. The stone is rolled away. Only grave clothes remain in an empty tomb. Something wonderful has happened! The bright morning sun gives new warmth on the faces of the worshipers as they expectantly greet one another in the church parking lot. In anticipation of this day the people have dressed in their finest. And the sanctuary is dressed in fragrant white lilies. An ugly, crude, handmade crown of thorns has been symbolically draped over the altar cross. The somber purple paraments have been replaced with brilliant new white ones. Yes, indeed, this Sunday is different! Christ is risen! He is risen indeed! Alleluia! Hearts are full of joy and thanksgiving because Christ has conquered death and made eternal life available to us all! What happens next takes place in thousands of Christian churches throughout the world, year after year. Even people who have not participated in congregational worship during the rest of the year come to church and join in the glorious celebration of this day. And what do they do once assembled? They stand and fervently give expression to the joy, praise, and thanksgiving that fill their hearts by singing "Christ the Lord Is Risen Today."

Congregational singing is one role of music in worship. Certainly there are other ways to praise God, but something about a congregation's singing its praise raises that expression to its highest level. We can know and experience the fervent and dynamic faith of the Wesleys when we sing "O for a thousand tongues to sing my great Redeemer's praise!" Music serves its purpose well when it allows the worshiper both individually and corporately to proclaim, "Then sings my soul, my Savior God to Thee, How great Thou art!" or "To God be the glory, great things He has done!"

Music and Proclamation

If Christ gave as his last instruction for the church to go into all the world and proclaim the good news (Mark 16:15), then music must have a role to play in that proclamation. The word *proclamation* might first bring to mind the image of the pastor preaching a sermon, expounding on a particular scripture text. There is in Protestantism a vital tradition of cultivating great preaching, great proclamation, of the gospel message. We often hear of "the centrality of the Word." But what we may not recognize is that music can play an important part in proclaiming that Word, as does preaching, and often with great effectiveness and profound impact on the hearer. John and Charles Wesley certainly recognized this.

Choral works as different as J. S. Bach's *St. Matthew Passion* and John W. Peterson's *No Greater Love* powerfully proclaim the message of salvation to the listener. The entire world, Christian and non-Christian alike, has heard the most basic and central tenet of our faith in a risen Savior through the singing of "I Know That My Redeemer Liveth" from Handel's *Messiah*. The soloist who sings Bill Gaither's "He Touched Me" is proclaiming that Jesus Christ can set one free from the burdens of guilt and shame, just as the pastor who preaches on the woman caught in adultery in John 8. Each Christian can share his or her own personal witness through singing the gospel hymn "I Know Whom I Have Believed," or they can together proclaim their faith by singing hymns such as "The Church's One Foundation."

Music can play an important role in carrying out Christ's Great Commission. It can assist the church in spreading the gospel as well as allow the individual to personally testify to his or her faith. Music can lead to effective evangelism.

Music and Education

Many pastors have preached many sermons to many congregations for the express purpose of teaching the fundamentals of the faith. Great sermons have educated the faithful on eternal life, the nature of the Trinity, the love of God, the mystery of the Incarnation, and other points of doctrine. Many Sunday school teachers and vacation Bible school leaders have instructed their young classes in the history, work, and beliefs of the church, the content and meaning of scripture, and what it means to live a Christian life. But despite our diligent efforts, how many worshipers can remember by Sunday evening what was preached or taught that very morning? An unfortunate reality is that those who hear sermons and lessons will likely forget most of what they have heard rather quickly. Of course, we pray that some of what is preached and taught will be retained and have an impact, for if it isn't, then our efforts are in vain.

Music can play an invaluable role in the educational aspect of worship. The worshiper may not remember the specifics of a sermon on the promise of God's grace, mercy, and forgiveness beyond the doors of the sanctuary, but millions of Christians have made the hymn "Amazing Grace" a part of their memory banks, securely and forever locked away in the very heart, mind, and soul of their beings. With little effort, they can sing one, two, or perhaps even five or six stanzas without stumbling. But more important, many of them could even teach a lesson on the promise of God's grace, mercy, and forgiveness, using the hymn as an outline.

Many adult worshipers will search the pew Bible in vain for the book of Ezekiel or 1 Peter, or will perhaps find it just in time to read along with the final verse of the morning's scripture lesson. But hundreds of little children would be able to find the text easily because a diligent choir director has taught them one of a number of excellent, singable songs which teach the names of the books of the Bible.

Choir members time and time again are pleased and amazed that somehow they can recite from memory large portions of the scripture lessons as they are read. The reason, of course, is that much of the best written and most sung choral literature is taken directly from scripture, as are the texts of many of the popular religious songs and choruses being increasingly sung in worship in recent years. Hundreds of outstanding hymns, choruses, songs, and anthems quote directly from or paraphrase scripture.

To make the best use of music in its educational role, pastors, musicians, and worship leaders will see that the music chosen for a given Sunday will reinforce and undergird the message of scripture and sermon. If the theme of Christmas Sunday's sermon is based on John 1:1-14, then the congregational hymn should not be "Angels We Have Heard on High." While it is part of the familiar body of Christmas carols and is much loved by the congregation, it does little to help explain the mystery of the Incarnation. How much more impact such a scripture reading and sermon would have when immediately preceded or followed by "Hark! the Herald Angels Sing," Charles Wesley's inspired musical commentary on the Incarnation.

Music and Ministry

On any given Sunday morning in nearly any Christian church, you can sit in almost any pew and be assured that at that very moment you are surrounded by persons of nearly every imaginable human condition. Two pews in front of you sit newlyweds Ray and Lisa Harrington, smiling, holding hands, overflowing with love for each other. Behind you is Clark Wilson. He retired this year after forty years of teaching high school math. He and his wife, Grace, were planning to celebrate by taking a trip to Hawaii this winter, but he's just been diagnosed as having terminal cancer. Down in front is Noelle Martin. She is bursting with pride at having just won the county spelling bee. Over there is John Breck. When he leaves the church after this morning's service, he will go directly to the nursing home where his wife has lived for the past five years. She has suffered from Alzheimer's disease for years now, and she doesn't understand who he is or why he has come to visit. And up in the choir sit Dale and Terri Hyland. A year ago their newborn son died in his crib without any apparent reason, and they have just learned that Terri is pregnant again.

The list could go on, but it remains strikingly similar in church after church. The congregation consists of people who cannot contain their joy and of many who struggle to go on living. There are people who are coping with emotional and physical pain and people for whom life is a celebration of happiness and success. Some will soon die, and some have just begun to live. But they are all participants in the drama of worship, and they come seeking expression to their various spiritual emotional conditions.

Just as music can be the vehicle for a congregation's expression of praise and thanksgiving on Easter Sunday morning, so can it touch each individual worshiper at his or her most immediate and compelling point of need. For the person who is approaching the end of life in this world with uncertainty and fear, "Because He Lives," "In the Garden," or "Amazing Grace" may provide a sense of assurance and confidence. For the person with cause for great celebration—a new baby, a marriage, a job promotion, a graduation, a championship football team—the music of congregation, choir, soloist, organist, or pianist can well express that inner joy as few other things can. For the family and friends who mourn the loss of a loved one, "I'll Praise My Maker While I've Breath," "Abide with Me," "It Is Well with My Soul," and many others can bring, not only comfort, but a realization that life for the Christian is eternal.

It is paradoxical that music in worship can allow a person both to express what is inside (sorrow, fear, doubt, anxiety, conflict, and joy) and to receive what is inwardly most needed at that moment (comfort, assurance, courage, hope, and peace).

For nearly twenty centuries Christianity has recognized the various roles of music in worship, and through diverse musical styles, methods, and practices, the church has worshiped and praised its Founder, proclaimed its message, educated its members, and ministered to their needs.

1
The Worship Leaders

Let us return to Kierkegaard's analogy of worship as drama. In staging any dramatic production, the two most important points to keep in mind are "Who is the audience?" and "Who are the actors?" Kierkegaard's answer is that God is the audience. God is the one watching and receiving the drama and the primary actors are the people of the congregation. The others—pastor, choir, music director, organist, pianist, and other worship leaders—are the supporting cast, "prompters," or the " stage crew" who enable the main actors—the people—to play out their role as worshipers. With this in mind, let us now look at the various roles of this supporting cast.

The Role of the Pastor

In many local churches, the pastor is the only person with formal education, training, or experience in matters of worship. Coupled with the pastor's responsibility for overseeing the worship life of the congregation, this makes the role of the pastor a most significant one.

As the person in charge, the pastor may reserve the responsibility for determining what happens in worship: sermon subject, scripture, prayer, hymns, acts of praise, and the order in which they come. In addition, the pastor may be the primary worship leader in the actual carrying out of these acts of worship. It is easy to see how in this situation the pastor may be regarded by the congregation as the focal point of worship. After all, he or she does the planning and leading for worship, as well as the actual performance of many things in the service.

1

For many, worship begins when the worshiper is seated in the pew and reads the bulletin. The pastor processes down the center aisle or mysteriously appears from some special, secret side door, and sits in the largest chair on the chancel. He or she then stands, proceeds through a call to worship or an invocation, announces and leads the opening hymn, and continues with a prayer or litany of confession, scripture, sermon, offertory, other hymns and prayers, and finally the benediction. The symbolism is not lost on the people when it is the pastor who gives the offering plates to the ushers and when it is only the pastor who receives the people's offerings and places them on the altar. In many churches, everyone is aware that it is only the pastor who presides over the service of Holy Communion, reading all the sections of the liturgy and perhaps even offering the elements to the people. It is the pastor who baptizes infants, children, youth, and adults. It is the pastor who receives new members into the congregation. In many churches, the role of the pastor is understood to be that of "chief worshiper," or to use Kierkegaard's model, that of "star actor."

But again, if we accept Kierkegaard's premise, then perhaps we should re-think the pastor's role in worship. If the people are the main actors—the main participants—in the worship drama, and if the rest are to be supportive, what can and should the pastor do to encourage this? What can the pastor do to be more of an "enabler" and "encourager" of worship rather than the focal point around which worship takes place?

The obvious answer is to encourage lay participation at all levels. In *Planning Worship Each Week,* Hoyt Hickman discusses many specific and useful ideas in this area. Briefly, here is a recap of some of his ideas and some others.

1. The more persons participate in worship, the more ownership they feel. Laypersons should be recruited, trained, and utilized in all

acts of worship—prayers, litanies, acts of praise, reading scripture, and others. Laypersons can and should take on responsibilities in worship beyond those of musicians and ushers.

2. Lay participation in the sacraments should be encouraged. Baptism and Communion are responsibilities to be administered by the pastor. However, the congregation will have a renewed interest and greater understanding of them if they take an active, participatory role. There is very little in the liturgy for these two services which must be done by the pastor. Everything else can be done by lay people.

3. Evangelical worship seeks to elicit a response from the worshiper, perhaps a renewed commitment to Christ, or a first-time decision to accept Christ as Lord and Savior, perhaps to unite with that particular congregation of Christ's church. But whatever the response a worshiper may be moved to make, laypersons from the congregation can and should be involved. That involvement may be a more symbolic lay involvement by having the lay leader assist in the receiving of a new person into church membership. A more dynamic involvement may occur if several members come forward with the prospective member as "sponsors" or "shepherds." Not only do they participate at the point of the person's decision or response, but they continue contact afterward to assimilate, encourage, and lead the new member into full and active participation in the life of the congregation.

4. Laypersons will find renewed meaning in and gain more from worship if they are involved, not only through participation in the actual worship itself, but also in the planning of worship. The pastor can utilize the talents of lay people in the worship work area during the earliest stages of planning worship. The same holds true in later evaluation of congregational worship. Who better than the

people can know the needs, aims, and expectations for their own worship?

5. Laypersons have a great variety of gifts, as do pastors. They can be put to good use in many areas related to worship. Obvious ones would include acolytes, ushers, and singing in the choir, offering a vocal or instrumental solo, or even forming or leading a choir. But others include the cleaning, care, and changing of the altar paraments and cleaning and polishing offering plates, the cross, and candlesticks. Some persons have talent in various areas of the arts—sewing, needlepoint, painting, making banners, designing worship bulletin covers, and performing drama and sacred dance. Others excel at growing or arranging flowers for regular Sunday morning use or for special occasions. The possibilities for lay participation in areas of the arts are many.

It takes more time, effort, and commitment for the pastor to serve as an enabler and encourager of worship rather than the central figure. But if worship is to be the most active, vital, nurturing, and meaningful thing a congregation does, then the pastor must assume the role of behind-the-scene director rather than onstage star.

The Role of the Choir

In worship, the role of the choir has three aspects. Everything the choir does should fulfill one (or more) of these three functions. These three functions are equal in nature and importance rather than hierarchical, and the choir fulfills its purpose best when these three are balanced. When one is given precedence, the effectiveness of worship is diminished.

First, the choir *leads* in worship. Some of the duties of the choir as worship leaders duplicate those of the pastor. For example, the pastor may begin the service with a spoken call to worship or a suitable verse of scripture. But this can also be accomplished musically by the choir singing one of the calls to worship provided at the back of most hymnals, a short excerpt of a choral selection, or a suitable stanza of a familiar hymn or chorus. The same can be said for many of the various portions of the service, including introits, responses before or after a prayer or scripture, and the benediction. The resources a choir can use as worship leaders are limitless, but the best resource of all is the hymnal. Hundreds of familiar stanzas and refrains lend themselves well for this purpose.

Second, the choir *assists, enables, and encourages* in worship. (As with the first role of the choir, the second sounds quite similar to the role of the pastor in worship. The reason goes back to Kierkegaard's model and its "casting" both pastor and choir in a role which supports the primary role of the congregation.) This role can take many forms, the most common and obvious perhaps being in promoting active and vital congregational singing. Hymn singing is *the* most physical and participatory activity of all congregational worship. It usually requires that the people stand, remove the hymnal from the rack, find the proper page, and engage their mental and physical faculties in unison with the other worshipers. It involves reading and considering the text. It requires special breathing techniques to sing the words, phrases, and musical pitches. It results in the worshiper, perhaps on a subconscious level, listening to the singing congregation and intentionally contributing and blending his or her individual voice with the whole. It brings a unity of action and purpose to a group of vastly different individuals. Finally, through singing the words of its songs, a congregation learns and expresses its identity, theology, history, mission, and faith.

We must treat with care and emphasis anything in worship that is so important, and here is one of the roles of the choir of which its members must continually be aware. The choir rehearses and prepares for its role of assisting the congregation in this important act of worship. The choir should never merely casually sing along with the congregation, perhaps improvising a harmony part, perhaps singing the right words, perhaps using the correct pitches. The choir, through careful and studious preparation, should be familiar with the text of the hymn and then sing the music in such a manner as to make the text clear. The congregation will imitate the manner in which the choir sings the hymns, whether that is casually and inattentively or carefully and purposefully. If choir members use their time of hymn singing to study the upcoming anthem, to concentrate on so-and-so's new outfit, or to ask another singer about the new persons in the back pew, then the congregation will likewise pay little attention to this important act of worship. (For the same reason, the pastor should always actively participate in hymn singing, with hymnal in hand, mouth engaged, and face expressive. The time for a last, silent read-through of the sermon text has long passed by the time a hymn is sung.)

What about choral descants and harmony on the hymns? Each choir and congregation should consider this matter individually. Some congregations will be encouraged and strengthened upon hearing the additional harmony parts and countermelodies sung by the choir, the result being exciting—even emotional (!)—worship in song. But others will only be distracted by the extra-musical elements, the result being confusion or timidity on the part of the congregation. The pastor, musicians, and choir members must be sensitive to the effect of their musical efforts in assisting congregational singing. If something has a positive impact, then do it. But if it does not, it is wrong to continue to do it because the sopranos like to sing descants or because the choir members are thrilled with their ability to produce beautiful choral harmony.

Not to be overlooked are the things a choir can do in worship which are not related to the music. Does your congregation make use of psalms, responsive readings, unison prayers, litanies, and scripture? Just as with singing hymns, the congregation will participate more actively in these actions if the choir participates fully and purposefully. Choir membership does not stop with the "Amen" after the hymn or with the choral benediction. It continues through the entire service and involves every worship activity. Choir members should continually be made aware of their role as enablers and encouragers of the worship of the entire congregation.

The third aspect of the choir's role is that the choir *ministers* in worship, just as does the pastor. Every member of the congregation comes with individual hurts, needs, and celebrations. One might be suffering physical pain. Another may be going through a period of doubt or a crisis of faith. Still another may be bursting with excitement and thanksgiving over something that happened that week. Or perhaps the congregation as a whole is going through some crisis or celebration and there is a commonly held need for the group to together share, sense, or express its common bond. Here are opportunities for the choir to truly minister to the congregation.

When the space shuttle Challenger exploded shortly after lift-off in 1986, the nation was shocked and numbed at the enormity of the tragedy. Our congregation felt as others in the nation the following Sunday. We struggled with the sense of loss and experienced the heartache felt by the friends and families of the crew. On that Sunday, our choir put aside the scheduled anthem and instead sang "On Eagle's Wings" by Michael Joncas (octavo #JO-01, North American Liturgy Resources, 10802 North 23rd Ave., Phoenix, AZ 85029), a beautiful and moving work based on Psalm 91. As the choir sang, "And He will raise you up on eagle's wings, bear you on the breath of dawn, make you to shine like the sun, and hold you in the palm of His hand," the congregation was reminded that even when tragedy strikes, when victory and joy are in an instant changed to seemingly comfortless loss, when our sadness becomes oppressive, that even then—and perhaps most especially in those times and circumstances—our assurance is that God will comfort, heal, and restore hope, and our spirits will be renewed. Singing this song was a compelling and memorable example of the choir in its role as minister.

The Role of the Music Director

The music director's role is often similar to that of the pastor and should evolve in close cooperation with the pastor. The pastor, sometimes together with the staff, the worship work area members, and other groups and individuals in the church, has the primary responsibility for congregational worship. The role of the music director often is determined by how large a role the pastor and others assume. But in most churches for most directors, the role will include some or all of the areas listed below.

Plan. Planning requires attention to a host of details: background and tastes of the congregation; size and content of the music library; the season of the church year; the lectionary; musicians available in the congregation; the music budget; potential for growth; musical instruments available; goals and expectations of the pastor and people. Planning must be a continual process and must be done for the *distant* future, the *foreseeable* future, and the *immediate* future. Few directors manage to squint their eyes and strain their minds to plan for three, five, or even ten or more years ahead. Some manage to plan for a season or a year, perhaps even two. Unfortunately, all of us have been in the position of having to change our plans for the immediate future, such as: "My two lead sopranos came down with the flu yesterday and won't be in church tomorrow morning; what number can I pull out of the files for the choir to sing?" But tragically, all too many directors never get beyond the stage of planning for the next week or month.

Lack of sufficient planning results in always feeling the pressure of meeting an immediate deadline. Sometimes the music director's need and desire to plan ahead are frustrated because the pastor does not plan ahead. Some pastors don't begin working on a sermon text or content until Monday or Tuesday before they are to preach it. Consequently it is difficult for the music director to plan much beyond that same schedule. Even worse, this results in a situation in which the congregation assembles for worship on Sunday and the pastor and music director have not done any joint planning. Horror stories abound of such cases, one common one being the service where the pastor preaches a communion sermon stressing the victory of Christ over death and the music director selects hymns reflecting Christ's suffering and the somber reflection that comes from the Last Supper. Continual and diligent planning will contribute to effective worship.

Recruit. As with planning, recruiting must be continual and diligent. Few people will join a choir on their own. Most people are not musicians, and many have had little or no musical training. What little they may have had was thirty years ago in the third grade and long since forgotten. The typical congregational mindset is, "O how wonderful the choir is. The members are so talented. I could never sing like that." Therefore, one role of the music director is to look and listen for potential choir members. Watch the congregation during the hymns. Who appears to be singing and enjoying it? Whose voice is that you hear singing bass in about the sixth pew? Who frequently expresses appreciation and encouragement to you for your musical efforts? But even beyond these few obvious leads to recruiting, you must believe that every member is a potential choir member, and then make positive, encouraging overtures to recruit even those who consider themselves not to be choir material.

Cultivate, Nurture, and Encourage. Remember that choir members require continual care and attention. They like to be commended when they have worked hard and prepared well. Nothing is wrong in praising musicians for their diligence and recognizing their service. Likewise there must be pruning, discipline, and correction. Firm leadership and direction, correcting errors and offering suggestions for improvement, result in precision and excellence.

Minister. It is with reason that the music directors who appear to be most successful in their duties are often called "ministers of music." Regardless of the size of the church, the number of choirs or choir members, or the predominant style of worship and music, music directors should adopt an attitude and approach to their task of "ministry." It calls for a sense of dedication to meeting the needs of their choir members and congregations through music. There is little room in church music *ministry* for the director interested primarily in self-fulfillment, demonstrating his or her own musical excellence as a singer or instrumentalist, or attaining a high salary or level of prestige. But there will always be a place for one who finds purpose and mission in using his or her own talents to share the message of love, mercy, and grace and to bring forgiveness to the lost and hope to those who have none. The minister of music is a shepherd to those in the choir, and along with the pastor, ministers to the needs of the entire congregation.

Evaluate. Perhaps with the pastor, the music committee or worship work area, members of the congregation, the choir as a whole, or perhaps alone, the music director must objectively evaluate the past in order to improve the future. It can be as simple as returning to your office or home after a service and reflecting on what worked best, what did not, and why. You must take into consideration things such as style, content, emotional impact, degree of congregational participation, and what people express to you in words, looks, attitudes, tone of voice, or body language. You may need to cultivate skills which will help you encourage feedback of pastor, choir, and congregation, and then be objective in your evaluation. There will be occasions when your evaluation will be one of "Well done, thou good and faithful servant." And there will be others of "Oops!"

Prepare. You may spend years practicing an instrument or taking vocal lessons. You may even attend a college or university to develop your skill to a high degree. You may search for resources through stacks and shelves of music in a store. Perhaps you will attend a seminary or take summer course work in theology, church history, and polity. Or perhaps you are the church music director because you are the only one who can play the organ or sing reasonably in tune with the piano. Maybe you have had no formal musical training, but you are willing to direct the choir or lead the children's choir because no one else will and you know how much the congregation will benefit if there is a choir. All of this is good. But you must realize that training and preparation never cease; despite all your training and efforts, despite your prayerful dedication and sense of ministry to others, you are never fully prepared. There is always more you can and should do as a music director. Certainly you must read books and articles. You must listen to recordings and attend concerts and other churches' worship services. You should attend workshops sponsored by your district, conference, or other groups, such as the General Board of Discipleship or the Fellowship of United Methodists in Worship, Music and Other Arts. You must spend time practicing your own instrument or vocal skills and perfecting your skills as director. But perhaps most important of all, you must devote considerable time to reflection, prayer, scripture reading, and study of the materials you ask your choirs and congregations to sing. Preparation is what you do as continuing education which keeps you qualified.

The director's role is a difficult one. The director must be sensitive to the needs, desires, tastes, and expectations of the congregation, the choir, and the worship or music committee and the pastor, while also being true to his or her own self. If you as the director believe that a high calling and long preparation for the task will avoid conflict and heartache, you will soon learn otherwise. If you believe that the importance of leading, assisting, and ministering in worship will only bring personal joy, satisfaction, and unending gratitude on the part of those with whom you work and serve, then you may be shocked or disillusioned when you discover that even Christians can be unfair, petty, and cruel.

To be sure, there are times of satisfaction and joy. There are occasions when the pastor will express thanks and gratitude for your hard work and invaluable contribution to worship and ministry. There will be Sunday mornings when Mr. Campbell, the lawyer, community leader, and strong pillar of the church, will come to you with tears in his eyes and thank you for the choir's anthem that morning. You won't know what is happening in his life which prompts his heartfelt expression, but you whisper a prayer of thanks to God for allowing you to have been an instrument of grace. There are even times when the congregation will express its appreciation for your service with a raise in salary. And if you are truly fortunate, someday you will have a conversation with young Dale Walters. As he sits across from your desk in your office, you remember the first week he came to sing in the children's choir and how you thought he had an unusually good sense of pitch. You recall the years he played handbells, the trips he took with the youth choir, and the many afternoons you spent together as piano teacher and student.

And later he looked so uncomfortable sitting in the choir loft in his long, flowing robe, the only teenager surrounded by adults the age of his parents. But now he sits in your office telling you he has decided to study music in college and hopes to become full-time minister of music . . . just like you!

But for every one of these, there will be other times of doubt, conflict, frustration, and disappointment. On occasion you and the pastor will disagree, perhaps heatedly, and unfortunate things may be said by either or both of you. There will be Sunday mornings when you have pulled together your full potential as musician and director and have brought the choir to its highest level of musical excellence, only to have Mrs. Putnam come to you after the service and say, "The choir certainly was *loud* this morning!" You will experience periods when choir membership will drop, or the members' spirits will seem depressed and you will be unable to revive them. You may see years when you selflessly give of your time and talent out of love for Christ and the church, and when the congregation will continue to allow you to serve without financial remuneration. Or perhaps you will go for years with no increase in salary as you watch the budget increase, apportionments go up, staff members added, and the pastor's salary raised.

Regardless of the church size, number of choirs, or amount of the budget, as music director you will experience periods of great satisfaction as well as bitter frustration and disappointment. You will know times of incredible closeness to God as well as times when you feel you have been forsaken.

But through it all—the good and the bad—your role is an important one. In the entire cast of the divine drama of Sunday worship, perhaps only the pastor has the position and means to minister to more people's needs than you. It is a high calling, indeed, and it demands dedicated commitment.

The Role of the Congregation

Mention has already been made of the all too frequent nature of the role many congregations are assigned, namely, that of spectator. In too many churches worship is a performance done *for* the people *by* the pastor, music director, and choir members. This kind of spectator worship is a passive activity, similar to that of watching a football game on television, with the announcers doing the play-by-play commentary, the band entertaining at halftime, the cheerleaders encouraging the teams, the coaches directing the play, and the players running, passing, catching, kicking, and blocking. And while all of this activity is going on, the viewer sits comfortably on the sofa and is entertained.

It does not take a large leap of imagination to see the pastor as coach and announcer, or the music director and choir as halftime entertainment, with the congregation comfortably seated in the padded pews as the successive plays of worship strictly follow the program of the printed worship bulletin. Occasionally the congregation may be called upon to stand and sing or respond in a litany, not unlike the role of the cheerleaders. But the question is: Is that the kind of vital, dynamic, life-giving, and sustaining worship we want?

In this chapter we have looked at the roles of the pastor, the choir, and the music director. Those roles, if properly understood and applied, will result in active rather than passive congregational worship, with the people as participants rather than spectators. But beyond this, there are specific things a congregation can do, both individually and collectively, to take on their role as lead actors in the worship drama.

Congregation as Choir. The congregation knows that the choir practices for its part in the service. One night each week for an hour or two, the choir comes together to prepare the music for congregational worship. If the congregation can adopt an attitude that it, on a larger scale, is a kind of worship choir, then its role is strengthened. Many church newsletters list sermon topics and scriptures and the hymns to be sung. How much more meaningful would worship be if the congregation read the scriptures, thought about them, and even read the hymn texts ahead of Sunday morning? This is how the worshipers can prepare for worship, with a kind of "congregation practice," similar to the Wednesday night "choir practice."

Second, the congregation needs to be encouraged to fully and actively participate in the service. An affirmation of faith or a creed is a way for the people boldly to proclaim their faith together—it must not be mumbled under their breath. The liturgy of Holy Communion is one way God visits each man, woman, boy, and girl individually. If it is observed only twice a year or if the only participation the people have is in consuming the elements, then it is no wonder our people look on it as a burden. It must be made to be celebrational, victorious, and energizing, and the people need to understand why and how it is properly observed. Then they will welcome it and eagerly join in the feast.

Hymn singing must be understood to be something every worshiper participates in, for it is in the joint raising of our hearts and voices in song that we direct our worship to the true audience— God. Through our singing we offer praise and thanksgiving; we repent of our sins; we express our concern for each other and the world; we proclaim the message of salvation; and we renew our commitment to Jesus Christ. You need only look briefly at a typical Sunday morning congregation during the singing of a hymn before you will see people who have no understanding or appreciation for the importance of adding their voices to the rest. If the congregation understands hymn singing to be the equivalent in importance and relevance to them as the anthem is to the choir, then its congregational song will take on a new and urgent importance. And if worship leaders devoted an appropriate amount of time and effort to encouraging and perfecting congregational worship through singing, as we do to choral singing, the spirit and vitality of congregational participation would be increased. The following chapter will deal with this in more detail.

Support, Encourage, and Undergird. Most pastors and music directors would agree that they covet few things more than the support and encouragement of the people they serve. There are many things a congregation can and should do which lead to more effective worship leadership. First and most important of all, the people can pray for the wisdom, guidance, and direction of God's Holy Spirit on those who do the planning and leading week after week, year after year. Pastors, directors, and choir members who know they are regularly upheld in the prayers of the people are strengthened and enabled in their own roles.

If the time comes when a more tangible form of support is requested, the congregation can respond with gifts of financial resources, time, and talent. Members can offer babysitting for the children of choir members preparing a special Christmas musical. They can volunteer to donate materials and their own talents to sew costumes for the children's musical. They can provide vehicles and serve as drivers to take the handbell choir or youth choir to local nursing homes as they seek to minister to those shut-ins. They can build dramatic props, work the lighting or sound systems, or provide refreshments for a choir concert. All of these things, despite the fact that they are not specifically an act of Sunday morning worship, show the appreciation and support a congregation has to offer its ministry of worship and music.

2
The Accompanist

This entire chapter is devoted to the role of the accompanist in worship for several reasons. While other worship leaders—pastor, music director, and even choir—play a more visible and certainly a more vocal role, there is no more important worship leader than the accompanist. The pastor or director can announce and vocally lead the congregation in the hymns, but the major responsibility for good congregational singing rests on the shoulders of the accompanist. The choir can fulfill its various roles in worship, but unless it is singing a cappella, success can be largely dependent upon the ability of the accompanist. More than one pastor will readily testify to the unfortunate occasion of a wedding in which the bride's Uncle Joe, who once looked at an organ, was asked to serve as organist, and nothing went right. He knew nothing of principles, mixtures, and reeds. The drawbars were a mystery. He couldn't understand why one manual wasn't enough for any organist. And consequently, the prelude was an unsettling experience to those present; the processional sounded like a circus march complete with calliope and lacking only the monkeys and elephants; and the soloist could not hear any hint of rhythm or proper harmony and could only guess at the appropriate moment to begin the next phrase.

The Role of the Accompanist

Of all the leaders of worship, it is the accompanist who possesses the potential to influence the ultimate success or failure of the worship experience. This truth escapes many pastors, directors, and even organists or pianists. We rely on music throughout our services, beginning with the prelude, a choral introit or call to worship, the opening hymn, a musical setting of a psalm, a prayer response, a second hymn, choir anthem or solo, musical offertory and doxology, a hymn before and after the sermon, a choral benediction or congregational response, and the postlude. The accompanist is critically involved in all of these.

Music moves the drama of worship along. It is music which sets the appropriate mood or tone. It is music which allows the congregation to be full participants in the service rather than mere spectators. To a large degree, music determines how successful a pastor is in fulfilling his or her role. On the other hand, music can also be an obstacle to worship. It can destroy the proper mood or tone. It can be an inhibiting factor to congregational participation, or worse yet, it can encourage the members of the congregation to expect to be mere observers in their pews as they are entertained by the pastor and musicians. And if the aims of the musicians or the accompanist and the pastor are not the same, the effectiveness of both are reduced. Clearly, music's role is a significant one, and the role of the accompanist is crucial.

One important role of the accompanist is to lead, encourage, and support congregational singing. In this responsibility the word *accompanist* is more properly understood in a context of "leader." It is important for the accompanist to first set the tone or mood of a hymn. If the congregation is to sing "A Mighty Fortress Is Our God" or "To God Be the Glory," the accompanist must convey the expectation that the congregation is to sing with strength and conviction by playing in a similar manner. These two hymns and other similar ones must be introduced with vigorous, rhythmic playing of a suitable volume and tempo so that when the congregation begins to sing, it will do so in a manner which is expressive of the text. Likewise, if the hymn to be sung is "What Wondrous Love Is This?" or "The Old Rugged Cross," the introduction of the hymn, through tempo, registration, volume, and expression, conveys to the people the manner in which they should sing, namely one of reverent thoughtfulness and contemplation rather than unbounded joy and praise. The accompanist who is not sure of what or how to play a hymn introduction contributes to a congregation's being similarly unsure of when to sing, what to sing, and how to sing. Hymn accompanying must never be tentative or halting, for congregations will quickly follow the leadership of the accompanist in how they sing. Confident playing leads to good singing.

Once the appropriate introduction has set the stage for singing, the mood must then be maintained throughout the hymn. If the accompanist drags the tempo, so will the singers. If the accompanist lacks rhythmic precision, the congregation will not sing together. If the accompanist plays softer as the hymn progresses, the people will sing progressively softer and with less strength. If the accompanist is unsure or tentative about ending one stanza and beginning the next, then the congregation cannot help but be the same. However, the accompanist who establishes and then continues a good tempo, who moves the music along with precise, rhythmic playing, and who is continually aware of the proper volume for a specific stanza will greatly contribute to the people doing the same. One of the great delights of accompanying congregational singing occurs when the accompanist first realizes the power that he or she possesses in contributing to and leading, even controlling the quality of, congregational singing, and the responsibility which goes along with it.

Another role of the accompanist is to accompany the music of other worship leaders, including the choir, a soloist, a quartet, an instrumentalist, or other musicians. It should go without saying that this role demands the accompanist be prepared to play the right notes. If all attention is focused on a soloist or the choir, wrong notes from the piano or organ can only be a distraction. But beyond the expectation of playing the correct notes, a good accompanist will play in a manner which keeps attention on the singer. The tempo, volume, and style of accompanying as well as the physical mannerisms of the accompanist should not call attention to the accompanist. They should contribute to the ability of the singer to convey the content of the text of the music. The accompanist should understand and cultivate a role of support rather than competition with the singer.

A third role of accompanist is that of soloist. During some occasions in the service, the organ or piano is played alone, including preludes, offertories, and postludes. If there is disagreement in this area, it is centered on whether such solo instrumental music truly contributes to congregational worship or whether it constitutes performance. Some would say that an organist who plays Bach's "Toccata in F Major" as the prelude is merely demonstrating the musical ability of the performer and the composer, and such performance has little or nothing to do with worship. However, others might say that such an offering constitutes a devout act of consecration of talent on the part of the organist and contributes to a spirit of praise and celebration on the part of the congregation. The attitude and practice of congregations, organists, and pianists will vary greatly on this issue.

Other portions of the service given over to solo playing might include a short instrumental chorus or hymn stanza in preparation for a pastoral prayer. Typically, the organist might play the refrain of "I Need Thee Every Hour" or "Sweet Hour of Prayer" quietly as the congregation and pastor still their thoughts and actions and wait upon the Lord in an attitude of quiet reflection.

Organ, Piano, or Both?

In one city there are two United Methodist churches, each with its distinct personality and worship style which have developed over the years. Church A is rather conservative. Many of its members are older, and the congregation is made up of well-to-do people who are leaders in the community. They recently elected to purchase a new organ for their large and well-appointed sanctuary and chose a large instrument by a recognized and respected manufacturer. The organ can accompany all the hymns and support the mostly classical and standard repertoire of the music program. Church A does not have a piano in the sanctuary.

Church B is not so conservative in style. Its membership is younger, with many families, young children, and teenagers. Theologically, it is the more evangelical of the two churches. The congregation especially enjoys singing a rousing gospel song or a modern praise chorus. Their style of Sunday worship is informal and free, at times charismatic. Hymn singing frequently involves guitars, drums, other instruments, and hand clapping. The church's organ is a two-manual spinet with one octave of pedals attached to two sound speakers. Congregational singing is supported by the organ and piano together. The choir and soloists may be accompanied by the piano, the organ, or both.

Both churches are comfortable with their use of piano and/or organ. Both churches are healthy, growing, vital, and committed to Christ. But church B cannot understand how the people in church A can worship with all that loud, stuffy, old-fashioned singing and that monstrosity of an organ blasting away so. And church A only shakes its head in amazement and bewilderment at the goings-on in church B. How, indeed, can one be expected to worship the Creator of the universe while the piano is pounding out an accompaniment which seems more suitable to a Saturday night hoedown?

The question of which instrument to use to accompany congregational singing—piano, organ, or both—largely depends on the history, make-up, and tastes of the congregation. Those who would argue for one or the other instrument fail to take into account other considerations such as performance practice and historical style. For instance, is it proper to accompany the singing of the beautiful Passion chorale "O Sacred Head Now Wounded" on the piano? The first answer is that if the piano is the only instrument available, then, yes, it is proper! However, if an organ is available, and if you wish to be true to the historical context of that hymn, and if you wish to support the introspective, contemplative nature of that hymn, then the organ is the preferred instrument. The percussive quality of the piano might be considered inappropriate or distracting in this instance. But what about "Blessed Assurance," "Victory in Jesus," or any number of spirituals or contemporary songs? The syncopations and dotted rhythms of these types of hymns are probably best accompanied with the percussiveness and rhythmic quality the piano provides. Any number of hymns could be accompanied by either or both piano and organ. Individual stanzas may make effective use of one instrument at a time, and others of both together. Further discussion of the various possibilities for accompanying hymn singing may be found in Chapter 4. Some claim that the two instruments, despite their similarities of keyboard, are tonally unsuited to being played together. Again, this is a matter of past practice, stylistic sensibilities, and taste of the congregation.

Pastors, music directors, choir members, organists, pianists, and congregations are not the same. They differ greatly, and the matter of "piano, organ, or both" must be decided individually. There is no single correct answer. Whatever choice you finally make will be the right one if it contributes to the best possible singing for your congregation.

Specific Musical Considerations
for the Accompanist

1. Who's in Charge Here? Picture a Sunday evening service. The congregation is attempting to sing "Standing on the Promises." The songleader has announced the hymn and is attempting to lead the singing, both vocally and physically. He wants the people to sing at a rather quick tempo. The organist, however, has his own opinion about the tempo; he believes that such revivalistic, camp-meeting style singing is not appropriate. Therefore, he uses the organ's resources of volume and tone to establish his own slower tempo and plays on with eyes glued to the hymnbook, totally ignoring the director. The pianist relishes this kind of hymn and uses it to exercise her abilities of improvisation by playing many full chords in the upper register interspersed with octave scale passages in the right hand and short rhythmic "riffs" in the left hand. She is in her own world, seemingly oblivious to the director and the organist. Then there is Sheila Carson, the strongest soprano in the choir and the lead soloist in the local community opera. She has her own idea of how the hymn should be sung and does not hesitate to demonstrate it at full throttle. The congregation, at the very least, is confused. Here is a reasonably familiar hymn, one which many in the congregation enjoy singing, but chaos reigns. Should they try to follow the director, the organist, the pianist, or the soprano? Should they just sing however they wish? Or should they put their hymnals back in the pew racks and give up? They can't be blamed if they opt for the latter.

The problem of "Who's in charge here?" is common to many churches, but it has a simple solution. Directors, organists, and pianists must continue to focus on their independent as well as their common roles as worship leaders. In their own different ways, each must strive to contribute to good congregational singing, and setting four different tempos is not accomplishing the goal. In some churches, the organist has considerable professional training and skill. In others, the director has, and in still others, the pianist. In some churches, two or perhaps even all three have considerable training. Musicians are notoriously temperamental, and church musicians are no exception. Until we have learned to control our temperaments and are willing to submit our individual tastes and sensibilities to the greater good of promoting vital singing, we are obstacles to and inhibitors of congregational worship. The solution is a simple one. There needs to be one tempo, one style of singing, and one leader. Perhaps that person is the appointed director, or perhaps that person is either the pianist or the organist. Perhaps that person is the pastor. In any case, there must be one leader, and the other musicians—instrumental or vocal—must follow. Anything else leads to confusion and chaos. If there is a songleader, the time and place to suggest an alternative tempo is not from the organ bench, halfway through the first stanza of a hymn.

2. Tempo. It was the annual Community Thanksgiving Service sponsored by the local ministerial alliance. The congregation consisted of Lutherans, Episcopalians, Roman Catholics, Baptists, Presbyterians, Methodists, and others. The host church's organist, known to be a competent organist, began the introduction to "All Creatures of Our God and King" at a rather slow tempo. By the end of the second stanza, the zeal and intensity of the "O Praise Him" 's were failing. The congregation was realizing that if the tempo continued to slow with each stanza, as it had the first two, no one would be singing by the sixth and final stanza. Many of us quit singing by the time we were halfway through the hymn, and marveled at the stamina of those who survived to the final "Amen."

As with many musical considerations, tempo can be a highly subjective thing. Different organists will choose different tempos, sometimes based on the practice of their own congregation. Some congregations are simply accustomed to singing faster or slower than others.

And yet, there is one suggestion accompanists and directors can use to arrive at a good tempo. First, read the text at a comfortable pace which allows for good, clean enunciation, clear phrasing, breathing at the proper places, and maximum expression of the text. Then attempt to sing the melody at approximately the same speed as you have just read the text. Usually this will give a good indication of the proper tempo for singing. Then accompany the hymn at that same tempo. There may be a need to adjust a bit faster or slower to take into account the musical aspects of the hymn, such as note values and meter (time signature), but it is almost always possible to set a comfortable musical tempo directly from a comfortable reading of the text.

3. Organ Pedaling. To trained organists for whom the pedals are no obstacle, the consideration of pedaling is simple. They know that there are occasions when pedaling is desired, and others when not. They know that when it is appropriate to play the pedals, the choice is to play detached or legato. They know the principles of varying accompaniment styles and how best to vary the pedaling technique. For instance, through six stanzas of "For All the Saints" (SINE NOMINE), there is ample opportunity to accompany singing without pedals (manuals only), with pedals legato, with pedals detached, and using varying pedal registrations, depending upon which stanza is being sung. But if your pedaling technique is less than professional, if you play only an occasional pedal, if you pedal with your left foot only, or if you are petrified at the mere thought of removing your feet from the resting crossbeam beneath the organ bench, then read on.

Most hymn settings are in four voices—soprano, alto, tenor, and bass. Ideally, the organist will play the bass line in the pedals and the other three in the manuals, with or without doubling the bass line. The first suggestion for the organist struggling with using the pedals is to get help. Find another organist in your area who will help you with technique. Set a time each week for a lesson and then work diligently on your own. Music stores usually carry a number of organ instruction books which will help you learn on your own if you wish. Perhaps your church would make available some continuing education funds for you to take formal lessons from a teacher or a college instructor. Their investment will more than pay for itself in the form of your increased effectiveness to lead and support congregational singing.

If additional study is not an option for you, some suggestions are listed. As you work at accomplishing these techniques, you may discover that by first learning these half-pedaling procedures, you may actually be well on your way to playing the entire bass line.

Important Note Pedaling. If you are unable to play the bass line in the pedals, go through the bass line and mark the most important notes. These may be the notes on the accented beats of the measure, the initial and closing notes of a phrase, or the notes which announce a change in harmony. They may include the notes on a significant word of text or a note which is longer in duration than the others preceding or coming after it. These important notes may or may not be the same for each stanza of the hymn. Once you have determined the most important notes, mark them in your hymnal and work at playing only those notes. Figure 1 of "Amazing Grace" (p. 27) shows the important notes circled which can be played in the pedals.

Tonic Pedaling. Analyze the harmony of the hymn. Regardless of the notes which appear in the bass line, play the tonic or root of the chord on the accented, important, or initial beats of the phrase, or

FIGURE 1

FIGURE 2

more often if possible. These notes sometimes can be sustained through changes of harmony in the manuals and sometimes not. Be careful to include the remaining harmony notes in the manuals. This technique is demonstrated in the example of "O for a Thousand Tongues to Sing" in Figure 2 (p. 27).

"Manual" Pedaling. This technique can closely approximate the sound of normal pedaling, but by playing manuals only. It will provide the low, fundamental support of the harmony which congregational singing needs. It should not be used in conjunction with either of the two techniques already mentioned. Set a registration on one manual which will give a strong low tone. If one of the manuals has one or more 16-foot stops in the manuals, this is the manual to use. If you have a 16-foot Swell-to-Great or Great-to-Great coupler, then use the Great manual. If the organ has identical sets of drawbars or similar pitch level tabs, experiment with different tonal combinations and choose the one on the manual which most closely approximates a good, low pedal sound when a single note is played at the bottom of the manual. When you have found the best "pedal" sound in the manual, play the entire bass line as written in the hymn with your left hand as low as possible on this manual. On the other manual, play the remaining voices with the right hand, using a normal registration for accompanying singing. This technique will work quite well on larger pipe and electronic organs, less satisfactorily on smaller organs. But no matter what kind of organ you have available, the result will be better than playing only the hymnal harmony's four voices in the manuals with hands together.

"Piano" Pedaling. If you are accustomed to using both piano and organ to accompany congregational singing, have the pianist play the bass line as a single note or as an octave in the lower register of the piano keyboard while you continue playing the organ manuals.

While not the same as organ pedaling, the lower range of the piano—especially if the bass line is doubled in the left hand—is quite capable of providing the low foundation tones required to support congregational singing. Another option would be to have another instrumentalist play the bass line for singing (cello, trombone, bassoon, baritone, etc.).

The Piano Accompanist. If you use only a piano to accompany congregational singing, remember that the bass line is important to support the harmony. Playing a hymnal setting as written will result in a weak and ineffective accompaniment, and the quality of singing will be affected. Try to duplicate the bass line in the left hand, playing the given bass note with the thumb and doubling it one octave lower with the little finger. All remaining harmony notes must be incorporated into the right hand. Figure 3 demonstrates this technique with "All Hail the Power of Jesus' Name."

FIGURE 3

4. Detached or Legato? Organists differ in their understanding of good accompanying technique. Some claim the proper style is a sustained manner, connecting notes and chords, even treating repeated notes as if they were joined with a tie. Pedal notes are played similarly legato, carefully connected and held to their full value. Repeated notes in the bass line are added together and played as if they were written as one long, sustained note. The second school of thought is just the opposite. Notes and chords are played in a detached manner. Repeated notes and chords in the manuals and pedal notes are articulated individually. Greater separations are made between successive phrases and hymn stanzas.

Organists are increasingly realizing that the latter manner of accompanying is best suited to support good congregational singing. Unlike the pianist, the organist cannot control volume and accent of the accompaniment notes and chords merely by playing the keys harder. The only way organists can do so is through attack, release, and duration of a note. A singer may sing the entire phrase "Standing on the promises of Christ my King" without stopping to breath in the middle of the phrase, but the smoothness and legato quality of the melody line are interrupted by the consonants of the words and the natural stress on the accented first beat of each measure. If the organist is playing in a very legato manner—connecting and slurring notes and tieing together repeated notes—this conflicts with or even works to defeat the rhythmic and percussive quality of the people's voices as they sing. But if the organist plays in a style which is imitative of how the voice sings the words and music of the hymn, then vocal singing is supported and encouraged. The best style to do this is the detached style described above.

It should be noted that organists often employ a technique of mixing the two different styles. Pedals can be played legato and manuals detached, or pedals detached and manuals legato. If the bass line being played is of an unusually melodic nature, as in "For All the Saints" or "Lift High the Cross," accompanying one stanza with contrasting styles between manuals and pedals is an effective means of providing variation to the accompaniment, especially in a hymn with five or six stanzas.

5. Volume. Remembering the unparalleled ability organists have to influence congregational singing for the better, volume is an important consideration. If the organist is timid, unsure, or afraid of making mistakes, he or she may very well play too softly. Perhaps additional practice will bring additional confidence. If the placement of the speakers is directly behind the organ console, the organist may be overwhelmed by the volume, with the result being inadequate volume for the rear of the sanctuary. If the organ is a large pipe or electronic installation, the organist may get caught up in the excitement, thrill, and joy of playing it and the resulting volume may be so loud as to cover up congregational singing. The organist must be familiar with the tonal resources of the instrument, the acoustics of the sanctuary, and the best way to support that congregation's singing. It is advisable for the organist to listen from all parts of the sanctuary as someone else plays the organ at various volumes and using various registrations. Unfortunately, in many of our churches, the organ bench is one of the poorest locations to adequately judge how loud or soft the organ really is.

6. Registration. Organs, organists, and congregations are so different that a few lines written here about registration can only be a beginning. If you are an organist who is confused with terms such as *principal, diapason, flute, reed, mixture, mutation,* and *chiff,* then you should borrow a book on organ history or registration from another organist in your area or the public library. Read it and try to apply what you read to the organ you play on Sunday morning. Most organs come with an owner's manual or instruction book which will explain the meanings of the terms on your organ stops and how to best use them. If one is unavailable, write to the manufacturer for a new one. For the beginning organist, some general observations may be helpful.

If your organ has tabs or drawknobs, they are probably grouped together in "families" of similar tone qualities. Some electronic organs use a uniform color for all stops within the same family. "Principals" are the foundation stops of the organ and should be the most relied upon for congregational singing. "Flutes" or "tibias" have a mellow and pleasing quality to them. "Reeds" imitate the reed and brass instruments, such as oboe, krummhorn, trumpet, and bombarde. Some organs may have additional voices such as strings or diapasons which may sound somewhat like a principal or a flute or a combination. "Mixtures" are combination stops of two, three, four, or even five different high pitch levels. They add brilliance and brightness to the registration. Some electronic organs also have a complement of "Percussion" stops for special effects such as chimes, bells, harpsichord, vibes, and the like.

Some of the stops will have numbers. These relate to the octave pitch level of that particular stop. Middle C played on an 8' stop is equivalent to Middle C on the piano. 4' on the same key will sound one octave higher, 2' another octave higher, and 1' yet another octave higher. 16' will sound the octave lower. "Mutations" are fractional stops, such as 5⅓, 2⅔, or 1⅗. These stops will produce a pitch somewhere between the octaves. You will need to experiment with each mutation on your organ to know exactly what it does. Organs with drawbars use this same numbering system, but many of them do not number the drawbars. Usually the drawbar on the extreme left is a 16' or 8' pitch. The second one may be a low mutation, such as 5⅓. The remaining drawbars will be different pitch levels on up the scale. Organs using a system of black and white drawbars use white for the octaves 8', 4', 2', and 1', and use black for the 16' and mutations, or partials. Some drawbar organs even have one or two at the right side of the drawbar grouping which will produce an upper mixture. Some of these same drawbar organs will also include preset tonal combinations on tabs. You must learn the sound of each of these and when to use them.

For normal congregational singing, try a registration of principals 8-4-2. Then experiment with what happens to the sound by adding additional principals 16 and 1 as well as the mutations and mixtures. Compare a chorus of flutes and/or diapasons, with and without mutations and mixtures. Then listen to both choruses with the addition of one or more reeds. Eventually you will discover what each organ stop sounds like and how to combine them for different uses of singing, preludes, responses, and solos. For a good, strong hymn of praise, try a principal chorus of 8-4-2 plus a mixture and one or more mutations. You might even add an 8' reed. For the final stanza, you can add a 16' stop and the 1' or a higher mixture. For a quieter hymn, reduce the number of stops and even experiment with using flutes or diapasons. Depending on the style of the hymn and the taste of your congregation, you might accompany one or more stanzas with tremolo or vibrato. While this would be inappropriate for "Come, Thou Almighty King," it might be fine for "In the Garden."

Good registration is that registration which best supports your congregation's singing. If that registration is a baroque principal chorus on a tracker action organ, then use it. If that registration is a complement of flutes and diapasons with tremolo, then use it. But make your choice of registration on the basis of congregational singing, not on your personal preferences or how they do it in the church across town or how you think Bach or Bill Gaither might do it.

7. Hymn Introductions and Interludes. There was a time when it was common practice for the organist to play the entire stanza and refrain of a hymn as an introduction. This is still the practice in many churches. But consider the purpose of the introduction. It is to announce the hymn, to identify the music of the melody the congregation is to sing, to establish the tempo, and to set the overall mood of the hymn. On Christmas Eve, can there be any reason to play an entire stanza of "O Come, All Ye Faithful" before the congregation sings? Of course, if the hymn to be sung is a new hymn or one with which most people may be unfamiliar, there may be reason to play it in its entirety as an introduction, but this is not the case for most of the hymns we sing in worship. Many organists prefer to play only a section of the hymn as an introduction.

What is played as an introduction is less important than *how* it is played. The best practice is to play the very opening phrase of the hymn rather than a later phrase or the refrain. This is because the congregation will begin singing the hymn if they have been reminded of the opening phrase. But it is more important for the organist to convey to the congregation the expected manner of singing with proper volume, tempo, registration, and playing style. A subdued registration, a tempo appropriate to the solemnity of the text, and a controlled volume will "telegraph" to the congregation how to sing the hymn "O Sacred Head, Now Wounded," just as a registration rich in principals and mixtures, a rather full and strong volume level, and a tempo which does not drag will prepare the people for the excitement and celebration of singing "Christ the Lord Is Risen Today."

Organists can make effective use in introductions of quite small melodic phrases or idioms found in the hymn. For instance, the first six notes of "O Come, All Ye Faithful" can be transformed into a fanfare-like figure and coupled with the closing phrase for a most

FIGURE 4

effective introduction. Figure 4 also demonstrates the technique of concluding the introduction on the dominant chord of the key rather than the tonic chord which makes the lead-in to the first words the congregation sings even stronger.

Some hymns, for reasons of emotional intensity of the text or simply of length, lend themselves to the incorporation of an organ interlude between stanzas. The folk hymn "What Wondrous Love Is This" is variously printed with two, three, or four stanzas, most hymnals having two. The hymn is not a particularly long hymn, but the emotional intensity of the text can be heightened and made more meaningful to the congregation if the organ plays a short interlude of six or eight measures between stanzas. This gives the congregation an additional moment to assimilate the words just sung before going on to the next stanza. Some hymns may even benefit from such an interlude after each stanza, including the last.

One excellent hymn to try this technique with is "Were You There." Other hymns are simply long hymns with many stanzas. If the congregation is to sing all seven stanzas of "All Creatures of Our God and King" or most or all of the seventeen stanzas of "O for a Thousand Tongues to Sing" in *The United Methodist Hymnal,* the physical requirements demanded of a congregation are such that their zeal and fervor may fail in the latter stanzas. A strategically placed organ interlude will give the singers an opportunity to catch their breath, regain their strength, and commit themselves anew to the task of singing through to the end. Interludes need not be great demonstrations of improvisational skills of the organist. Individual phrases or longer sections of the verse or refrain will serve well as interludes.

8. Modulation and Varied Accompaniments. One technique available to the organist who seeks to provide variety in accompanying congregational hymns is to use varied hymn accompaniments. These are published arrangements of hymns which alter the harmony and occasionally the rhythm. They are most commonly reserved for the final stanza of a hymn, but this need not be the case. They can be played with a contrasting registration, a broader tempo, and a heightened volume, all of which may serve to increase the strength of congregational singing. Some organists also make use of changing the key for one or more stanzas of a hymn, usually the last. Most modulations raise the key a half or a whole step, but others lower the key. The ability to change to a key other than the one printed in the hymnal can be learned through study and practice, or you can consult other hymnals to find the same hymn in a different key. Many varied accompaniments are written in a different key. If you make use of such arrangements, be careful to prepare a modulation which will lead the congregation to the new key. Never begin a stanza in a new key without making a musical transition to the new tonal center. Other instrumentalists would also appreciate knowing beforehand when such a modulation or altered accompaniment is to occur.

There are dozens of published volumes of these varied accompaniments and modulations between keys, some of which include additional musical parts for a choral or handbell descant, one or more trumpets or other instruments, or an added piano score. Some hymnals include varied accompaniments within the pages of the hymnal, and others, including *The United Methodist Hymnal,* publish a companion volume to the hymnal.

All of these musical considerations—tempo, pedaling techniques, detached or legato style, volume, registration, introductions and interludes, and modulation and varied accompaniments—are tools of the accompanist's craft. Perfecting them is not enough. It is more important to know how and when to use them.

Two questions must be asked in making that judgment: 1) Will it contribute to better singing? and 2) Will it help the singers to better express the text? As an example, consider the third stanza of "How Great Thou Art," which speaks of God sending his only Son to die on the cross and bear our sin. This stanza marks a drastic change from the powerful repetition of the preceding refrain's "How great Thou art!" A change in tempo, playing style, and registration can result in a similar change in the congregation's singing and can lead them to a heartfelt and genuine personal experience as they sing those important words. An additional tempo, style, and registration change can propel them along into the joy, affirmation, and celebration of the refrain and final stanza.

These musical elements used by the organist can greatly contribute to his or her being an effective leader of worship. The committed organist studies, practices, perfects, and then properly incorporates them into the worship drama.

3
Teaching Congregations to Sing

We have seen how the primary role of the pastor, choir, director, and accompanist is to lead and enable the congregation to worship. We spend considerable time, effort, and money training our worship leaders to do this. And yet the worshiping congregation is like the proverbial horse which can be led to water but can't be made to drink. The stage can be set, the actors in place, the lines rehearsed, and the crowd assembled, but when the curtain on the worship drama is drawn, something goes wrong. Despite all our planning, preparation, and best of intentions, our Sunday service may turn out to be a "flop." What went wrong? The pastor delivered a fine sermon which proclaimed the truths of the faith and the need for salvation and renewal. The choir had diligently rehearsed the anthem and did its best to lead the hymn singing. The organist's accompaniment was inspiring and supportive. The director did a fine job of selecting hymns and service music which supported the sermon text and season of the year. There were numerous opportunities in the service for silent meditation and individual prayer and reflection, corporate praise, confession, and thanksgiving. So why did the service seem lifeless and bland?

One answer may lie in the all-too-common fact that the congregational portions of the service, perhaps especially the hymns, do not engage the people completely and wholeheartedly. Congregational singing, instead of being entered into in a spirit of joyful abandon and unreserved commitment, is often dull, hesitant, self-consciously restrained, and meaningless. We ignore Wesley's charge to sing lustily and with good courage.

One reason for this poor state of affairs is that we have gotten

away from a proper understanding of congregational singing. For a
long time we have stressed the importance of having trained musical leadership to recruit, train, and direct our choirs. We have spent
so much time and so many resources in building and maintaining a
fully graded choir program and numerous handbell and other
instrumental resources in the church that we have short-changed
the people in the Sunday morning pews. Even worse, our efforts
have perhaps resulted in sending the message to the congregation
that music in worship is best done by those specially selected and
trained for it—the director, the soloist, the organist, the pianist,
and the choir. These are the people who fully enter into hymn
singing, even to the point of it nearly becoming a performance and
the congregation expecting to sit comfortably in the pews and
watch and listen to it. We talk about "special music," and even write
about it in the church newsletter hoping it will increase Sunday's
attendance. Are we on the way to converting Sunday worship from a
participatory to a spectator gathering? Poor congregational singing
is one result of misplaced priorities of worship leaders.

In this chapter we will look at some of the obstacles to vigorous
and vital congregational singing and steps to removing them, as
well as some positive steps which can be taken to make hymn
singing an exciting and vital part of worship.

1. People don't enjoy singing unfamiliar hymns. Nothing will
put a damper on a congregational singing like selecting a new and
unfamiliar hymn and expecting the people to sing it with the same
fervor and feeling as "Amazing Grace." We can wish all we want that
our congregation will relish the experience of learning a new hymn
and devote their full faculties to it in Sunday worship, but wishing
will not make it so. People want to sing the hymns they have known
and sung for years. They want to sing their favorites. They want to
sing the hymns which have some emotional and spiritual attach-

ment with their past. Faced with this set of circumstances, the pastor or music leader has two choices: continue to sing the same forty or fifty hymns the people have sung for years, or find ways to introduce new hymns into the repertoire.

One way to introduce a new hymn is to use it in the service for purposes other than congregational singing. The organist can play a published setting of it as a prelude or offertory. It may even be suitable to play the simple hymnal harmony with little or no elaboration. The choir might use the hymn as a response before or after a prayer, a call to worship, a benediction, or an offertory response. Have a soloist or duet sing the hymn for an offertory, or perhaps a choral setting is available as an anthem. The pastor may be able to use the text of the hymn in the sermon. The creative director can find ways to use the hymn in two or three successive services before the congregation is ever asked to sing it. Then when the congregation is to sing the hymn for the first time, it is not completely new to them. The members will recognize the organist's introduction as something familiar. They may remember the words from the choir's anthem the previous week or having been quoted in the pastor's sermon.

The director can do much to overcome a congregation's initial resistance to learning new hymns by saying something like the following before the hymn is sung: "This morning we sing a hymn which this congregation has never sung before. However, you have heard the words and the music a number of times played and sung by the organist and choir, so they will not be totally new to you. This hymn is based on the morning's sermon scripture text, and it will prepare our hearts and minds for our pastor's message." This kind of introduction can effectively overcome several obstacles to singing new hymns. It says plainly and honestly that the congregation is about to sing a new hymn. It informs the people that they have heard the words and music before, and the pastor considers it worthy enough for inclusion in the sermon. And it tells them the all-important *why* the hymn is being sung and why one of their old favorites may not be suitable. With this kind of preparation and encouragement, a congregation will more readily accept and may even come to enjoy learning new hymns. It takes time and coordination on the part of the worship leaders, but these efforts are well-rewarded with an enlarged hymn repertoire.

Once a new hymn has been introduced, sing it again. If it is worth learning and singing the first time, then sing the new hymn again the following Sunday or within a couple of weeks. Repeat it again a month or so later, and then a few months after that. If a new hymn can be used three or four or more times the first year, it is no longer a new hymn. It may even become one of "our" favorites.

2. Congregational rehearsal. How would your choir react if you presented the music for the anthem while the organist played the introduction to that anthem at the moment it was to be sung in the service? Somewhere there may be a choir which would enjoy the challenge and rise to the occasion, offering their best sightreading abilities, and then in the choir room after the service as they removed their robes and turned in their music, they would say, "O my, wasn't it wonderful to sing that new anthem this morning that none of us had ever seen before!" If this is the kind of reaction you could expect from your choir under these circumstances, then count your blessings! However, it is far more likely that most choirs would react by giving you expressions of terror as they listened to the new music of the organ introduction. Some of them might be able to sing some of their notes properly, or some of the words on the right beat, but most would struggle. There would be no hope of musically expressing the text. There would be no change in tempo or dynamic levels. If there is a repeat, a D.S., or a coda, expect utter frustration and embarrassment on the part of the singers. After the service in the choir room, you can expect to bear the brunt of their wrath. And don't expect to see some of them the following week!

No director alive would dare place faithful choir members in this situation. Yet we do it time and time again with our congregations. How can we expect the singers in the pews, most of whom are untrained, to do what we would never expect our trained choirs to do? We select a new hymn, often with more difficult melodic lines and rhythms and more challenging contemporary harmonies than the typical familiar gospel song, and then shake our heads in amazement when Mrs. Phillips closes her hymnal and slams it in the rack before the end of the first stanza, or when Mr. Carroll says after the service, "I certainly hope you never have us sing *that* hymn ever again! Can't we sing 'How Great Thou Art' once in a while?"

It is not reasonable to expect them to sing new hymns well and to enjoy it. One answer is to treat the congregation in the same manner as we treat our choirs: Have a rehearsal! In many congregations, the time before the service actually begins—the "gathering" time—is a time to visit and exchange greetings. But occasionally this time could be used to rehearse the congregation in a new hymn being introduced that morning. Bring the choir in early, and have the organist and/or pianist prepared. If both instruments are to be used, have the organist play the accompaniment in a simple and straightforward manner, with no alterations or embellishments, and have the pianist double the melody in octaves. Have the director move to a lectern or even a portable music stand down in front of the first row of pews. Then treat the congregation as though it were the choir. Have the accompanist play the hymn through once; then point out any unusual melodic skips or rhythmic difficulties. Point out the importance of the text. If necessary, lead the congregation in shorter phrases or sections before singing the entire hymn. Don't be afraid to repeat sections which need additional emphasis. Make corrections, but be encouraging. All of this can be done within five minutes. And when it comes time to sing that hymn in the service, take your place at the lectern or pulpit and physically direct the congregation in the hymn just as you rehearsed them. They will follow you just as the choir does. The result will be that you have added a new hymn to the repertoire. One final suggestion: A word of appreciation or encouragement from the pastor at some point in the service for everyone's extra efforts in learning the new hymn will contribute to the congregation's acceptance of learning new hymns.

Similar rehearsals can be held for new congregational responses or liturgies. Use this time and method for introducing a new chorus, hymn, or excerpt of a choir anthem to be sung by the congregation in succeeding weeks as a benediction. Some churches use this method for learning new musical settings of the Communion liturgy.

3. The varied use of hymns in worship. It is certainly desirable for the hymns in a service to relate to the sermon or its text. The proclamation of the Word is central to our worship, and the music of worship, specifically the hymns the people sing, should support this. However important preaching is in worship, it is only one act among others, and hymns can be used to relate to or even replace other acts of worship.

Choirs often are given the responsibility for moving a service along musically, as with the call to worship, introit, call to prayer, a choral amen, an offertory response, or a choral benediction, and there is no shortage of choral music specially composed for this purpose. However, a congregation could fulfill the same role quite effectively through the use of one or more stanzas of a hymn, a chorus, or even a familiar song. If the service calls for a period of silent confession before the pastoral prayer, have the congregation sing one stanza of "Dear Lord and Father of Mankind" or a similar hymn. (If the hymn is in public domain, print the stanza's text in the worship bulletin rather than having the people shuffle hymnals during the prayer.) Other prayer hymns might include "Father, I Adore You," "Spirit of the Living God," and "Seek Ye First the Kingdom of God." Such hymns and songs can be used effectively before or after prayer.

It is becoming increasingly common at large and festive gatherings to use Malotte's familiar setting of "The Lord's Prayer." Soloists and choirs have sung this setting for years, but now it is being sung by congregations. It has even been included as a congregational hymn in some newer hymnals. Most people have heard it at weddings and services and are sufficiently familiar with it that it could be used as a congregational response or song in a Sunday service. Some directors would be inclined to simplify and abbreviate the original accompaniment, but don't! The people know the music and will feel cheated if they don't get to sing to it. Have the accompanist play it in its entirety. And have the director physically lead the congregation as a choir. In addition to it being a moving worship experience for the people, it places this congregational favorite back in the hands and voices of the people rather than a soloist, as Christ intended.

Other individual acts of worship, typically done by the choir, can also be done by the congregation with a hymn. "Break Thou the Bread of Life" (which is *not* a Communion hymn) works well before or after the reading of scripture. Other hymns to varying degrees are related to specific scripture passages, some even being verse-by-verse renderings. Hymns before, after, or even during the offertory can reflect not only the giving of tithes and offerings, but also the consecrating of our lives to Christ. Most hymnals include a section of stewardship hymns and hymns of consecration or dedication. Some examples include "All Things Come of Thee," "Bless Thou These Gifts," Andrae Crouch's "My Tribute," "All to Jesus I Surrender," and "Now Thank We All Our God."

In many congregations the Doxology is sung as the conclusion to the offertory as the people's offerings are brought forward, placed on the altar, and consecrated to God, and most congregations use the familiar *Old Hundredth* tune. There are, however, many doxological hymn stanzas which could serve this purpose just as well and provide variety in the service. The topical index in a hymnal may include a section of hymn doxologies, typically the last stanza of a hymn. Another practice is to use the familiar "Praise God from Whom All Blessings Flow" text to a different tune. *Duke Street* and *Truro* work well. At Christmas, the text could be sung to the tune of "The First Noel," followed by the refrain "Noel, Noel . . . Born is the King of Israel." Avery and Marsh have an especially effective and exciting contemporary setting of the Doxology coupled with a longer Amen. Many congregations have used the tune *Lasst uns erfreuen* ("All Creatures of Our God and King") with its "O praise Him" and "Alleluia" refrain. During one recent service planned and led by the youth of the congregation, the people sang a spirited Doxology to the tune of "Hernando's Hideaway" from the Broadway musical "Damn Yankees."

4. Intergenerational singing. Singing is an activity which cuts across all lines and barriers, including age, sex, race, economic situation, occupation, and others. It is one activity in worship which serves to unite all individuals into one body—the Body of Christ. Worship should fully involve all of the individuals, and singing is one activity which accomplishes that despite age. Plan to incorporate hymns and songs which will appeal to all age groups, from the youngest child to the most mature adult. Songs can include "Yes, Jesus Loves Me," Avery and Marsh's "We Are the Church," and a host of children's favorite choruses and youth favorites such as "Pass It On" and "El Shaddai," all appropriate to congregational worship. It is obviously easier for adults to sing songs intended primarily for young worshipers than for young children to grasp the meaning of hymns not written for this age level. Time should be given over in Sunday school, vacation church school, and children's choir rehearsals to learn not only children's songs, but adult songs. The songs sung by the worshiping congregation should recognize and reflect the fact that the congregation is composed of all ages.

5. Hymns in special services. In many sections of the worship service or in some special or occasional services, congregational participation is limited or even nonexistent. The congregational role in baptism, confirmation, and reception of new members is often limited to a short, spoken response at the conclusion of the liturgy. It is even less in the typical wedding, funeral, or memorial service. Hymns can and should be included in these services to affirm the role of the congregation in these all-important life experiences. The topical index of the hymnal will include appropriate suggestions.

Other services or special occasions can also include congregational singing, such as dedication of a building or a new piano or organ, ordination, acceptance of a new or returning pastoral appointment, and patriotic or other topical services.

6. The acoustical environment. Given the importance of worship music in general and congregational singing in particular, it is difficult to understand why we design our houses of worship as we do. We want the voice of the preacher to boldly proclaim the Word of God for all to hear. We want the softest strain of the organ prelude to be heard by every worshiper, even in the back pew and the remotest corner of the sanctuary. We want the congregation to be encouraged and emboldened to sing the hymns with strength and conviction, not with timidity and hesitation. We want the organ and choir to resound in praise to the glory and majesty of God. And yet, what do we do? Many of our sanctuaries are designed with little or no attention paid to the acoustical requirements for vital worship and music. We design long, narrow rooms of worship where the congregation is far-removed from pastor, musicians, and worship leaders. We make extensive use of sound-absorbing materials in the walls and ceilings. In the interest of comfort we place plush padding and upholstery on the pews, or worse, install thick-cushioned theater-style seats for the congregation to occupy. We place arches, draperies, wall hangings, and other obstacles on the interior room surfaces to obstruct the sound. But worst of all, we cover the floor with thick wall-to-wall carpet. It is as if we are saying: "We will do what we can to teach, lead, and encourage worship through music and congregational singing, but it is more important that we worship in a physically beautiful and comfortable room. Visual aesthetics and physical comfort are more important to worship than acoustical considerations."

When we discover that worshipers in the rear cannot hear the soloist or understand the words of the preacher or choir, when we discover that congregations sing timidly and meekly rather than strongly because they become frightened at hearing only their own voice, when the sound of the organ becomes so flat and lifeless that it cannot possibly be an aid to congregational singing, that is when we take drastic steps to overcome our lack of acoustical planning for worship. That is when we bring in the sound technicians and acoustical engineers and are told that the solution to our problems will be to install an expensive sound system of microphones and speakers so that the people can hear the pastor, musicians, and worship leaders. And never mind trying to encourage each individual worshiper to sing boldly; that will require a complete renovation of the physical layout and design of the sanctuary.

So what is the solution? The answer is that for many of us, there is none. We learned too late that ideal worship acoustics do not include plush padding, carpeting, narrow sanctuaries, and sound-absorbing walls. And we must settle for makeshift solutions offered by electronic sound systems. But for others of us, we need to plan ahead. We must let it be known that good acoustics for worship do not simply happen. We must plan for them as we design our churches and sanctuaries. Consult an expert in that area before accepting any architect's recommendation. Better yet, consult the sound expert and make those requirements known to the architect before any plans are drawn. We must do this if we are serious about encouraging vital worship and song.

7. Varieties of hymn singing. Congregational singing, when done week in and week out, year in and year out, especially if there is a limited number of hymns repeated over and over with few new hymns introduced, can become stale, unexciting, and bland. But this need not be so. There is a limitless number of possibilities for varying how a congregation sings, and some of them are listed.

a. Unison Congregation. The typical congregation is not made up of musically trained singers, and nearly all of them will sing the melody. It is the melody which is familiar to them, and in fact, it is often the melody which is first associated with a hymn rather than the text. During the course of a hymn's three, four, or more stanzas, some stanzas may lend themselves to elaboration with choral descants, alternate organ harmonizations, or the inclusion of additional instruments such as brass, percussion, handbells, or others. The choir can sing in unison with the congregation or can add additional harmonic support by singing in parts. Accompaniment can be provided by piano, organ, or both. There might even be an occasion to have the congregation sing a capella, without instrumental accompaniment. Some churches do this every week and on every hymn! But most of us would use this technique only occasionally, and on hymns which have a chant-like quality, such as "Let All Mortal Flesh Keep Silence," "Of the Father's Love Begotten," or even one such as "Were You There When They Crucified My Lord?" The choir should know beforehand whether to sing in parts or unison. One result of completely unaccompanied unison singing is that the people will concentrate their attention more on the text, perhaps because there are no musical distractions. On a familiar hymn with simple harmonies, many congregations, especially with choir leadership, could sing some of the parts.

b. Responsive Singing. In this variation of congregational singing, the congregation alternates singing with another group of singers, an individual—such as a soloist, the director, the choir— or even the instruments. The most natural occasion for responsive singing might be a "dialogue" hymn, such as the first stanza of "Are Ye Able," in which a soloist or choir may sing the verse and the people will respond with the refrain. Another technique is illustrated in the Christmas hymn "How Great Our Joy" in which the congregation would sing most of the hymn and a quartet or the choir could sing the sections marked "echo." This responsive technique is also effective in the singing of many of the Negro Spirituals which use the call-and-response pattern. Examples include "Down by the Riverside," "Certainly Lord," and "There's a Meetin' Here Tonight." *Songs of Zion* and *The United Methodist Hymnal* abound with others. Responsive singing as well as antiphonal singing are two of the methods of Psalm singing utilized by Christians and Jews for centuries. As Psalm singing gains in popularity in our churches and comes to replace the use of nonmusical responsive readings, make use of both techniques.

c. Antiphonal Singing. Antiphonal singing is similar to responsive singing, except that the congregation is divided into one or more groups for singing rather than singing as a whole juxtaposed to a soloist or the choir. The congregation may be divided along many different lines, including physical location (front/back, balcony/knave, left side/right side). Other groupings may include male/female, children/youth/adult, or over 40/under 40.

d. **Nonmusical Hymns.** This may seem a contradiction in terms, but consider the fact that the most important element of a hymn is the text. To say that a hymn is well-written means that the musical elements of melody, harmony, rhythm, and style serve to make the textual meaning clearer to the singer. Occasional use can be made of the congregation reading in unison one or more stanzas of a hymn. This takes the text completely out of its musical setting and often results in a renewed understanding or heightened awareness of the hymn's message. Some hymns, especially those which were originally penned by the author as poetry, are effective if read in their entirety rather than sung. A related technique, through choir leadership, instructions from the song leader, or printed direction in the worship bulletin, is to encourage the people to speak in a manner which best expresses the emotion of the text. This can be done through changes in volume, speed, and spoken pitch level.

Aside from this technique's advantage of aiding in understanding and expressing the hymn text, there is a very practical benefit of time. Some hymn stanzas are never sung because there are simply too many of them. One song leader remarked that there is nothing worse than being a third stanza of a four-stanza hymn in an evangelistic song service. Less time is required to read or speak a hymn than to sing it; therefore, speaking it will allow you to recite all stanzas of a hymn which might normally be abbreviated.

e. **Silent Hymns.** As with nonmusical hymns above, this seems to be a contradiction in terms. However, hymns provide an exceptional opportunity for silent individual meditation or devotion. Many hymn texts or individual stanzas express just the right thought or emotion required at a certain point in the service. The congregation can be directed to read one or more stanzas silently while the accompanist plays. The same suggestion may be made to the congregation at the start of the prelude. Some worshipers use this gathering time to meet and greet others, and what might be a quiet, meaningful act of worship is transformed into something resembling the chaos of a family reunion. A printed direction in the worship bulletin may encourage people to enter the sanctuary quietly and use the text of one or more of that Sunday's hymns as a meditation to prepare themselves for worship.

f. **Authentic Performances.** Each congregation will develop its own preferred style of hymn singing. It may change some with the coming and going of pastors, accompanists, directors, choir singers, and members of the congregation, but the accustomed manner of hymn singing will remain remarkably the same over a period of years. One church is invigorated by singing at a tempo so quick that it would leave another congregation breathless. Another church prefers slower, broader tempos. One congregation may seldom sing gospel hymns, but another may thrive on them. However, regardless of the musical taste and sensibilities of the congregation, one way to introduce variety in hymn singing is the occasional use of "authentic" hymn singing, that is, singing a hymn or a stanza in the manner in which it was originally sung, or adapting a hymn to a style different than the accustomed style of your congregation. Sometimes this technique may be done by the congregation, other times by the choir. Different methods will require different musical skills. Here are some examples.

(1) **"O Come, O Come, Emmanuel."** This frequently sung Advent hymn, when sung in the same regular rhythmic manner as are most hymns, would be strange indeed to the church of centuries ago which gave us this hymn. It was originally sung as a chant, without accompaniment and with irregular patterns of rhythmic groupings based on the text. The quarter notes and half

notes are much more recent additions. In an authentic performance of this hymn, the words are grouped together in phrases of inexact note values. As the melody rises, the voice is raised in volume and intensity. As the melody descends, so do volume and intensity. The voice accents or slightly lengthens important individual words within a phrase. Individual words and phrases are used to determine how to sing the notes. Tempo is inexact. As the phrase progresses, the tempo may quicken a bit and then trail off as the phrase concludes. There is a slight lengthening of the final note of the phrase—a breath—and then the singers proceed to the next phrase. All voices sing the melody without harmony. Instruments, if used at all, should double the melody, and accompanists should closely follow the leading of the director. Effective use may be made of an organ "pedal point," that is, a long-sustained note in the pedal which would provide a single fundamental note for one or more phrases. The refrain of this hymn is quite properly sung in a more traditional manner with regular rhythm and note values, with harmony and with accompaniment if you like. Other hymns which can be sung in this chanted manner include "Let All Mortal Flesh Keep Silence" and "Of the Father's Love Begotten."

(2) "On Jordan's Stormy Banks I Stand." This is a good hymn to illustrate the technique of text painting. The opening stanza of this hymn speaks of standing on a stormy riverbank, casting "a wistful eye" on fairer worlds afar. The hymn abounds with images of a better life after this one, so the singer is longing for the peace and joy of heaven. A wonderful ethereal, dreamlike sense is created in this hymntext, yet we sing it in a rousing manner as we might sing a gospel song or a great spiritual. Worse yet, many hymnals print this hymn in a major tonality rather than a minor tonality. On one or more stanzas, encourage the singers to adopt a mood of wistful longing and quiet reflection, and sing it in the parallel minor key

rather than the major key. Accompaniment is optional.

Text painting can also be used in the hymn "How Firm a Foundation." The opening stanza speaks of the Word of God as a firm foundation of our faith. Have the men sing the words of this stanza on a unison low G, resulting in a vocal "pedal point." Or the basses and tenors could divide and sing an open harmonic fifth of G and D. Above the men's voices, the women sing the melody as printed. The result is that the music "paints" the text for that stanza.

(3) "What Wondrous Love Is This?". This United States folk hymn could be adapted to authentic performance in a number of ways. One is to bring out the open quality of the harmonies. This means that some of the harmonies are incomplete, lacking the third of the chord. Singing the hymn in unison but accompanying in incomplete triads is one method. Another would be to divide the choir into two parts, with sopranos and tenors singing the melody and altos and basses singing the melody a perfect fifth below, resulting in completely parallel fifths. This device should be used sparingly, perhaps for a phrase or two, but for no more than one complete stanza. Still a third technique, one which is entirely adaptable to congregational singing, would be to divide the congregation into two groups. Have one group sing the first phrase, "What wondrous love is this, O my soul, O my soul," and sustain the word and pitch of the final note ("soul") while the second group goes on to sing the second phrase, "What wondrous love is this, O my soul." The second group in turn sustains its final word and pitch as the first group goes on with the third phrase, and so on to the end of the stanza.

(4) Reformation Chorales. The period of the Protestant Reformation produced an enormous number of congregational hymns, called "chorales." Today much of this music is heard only in a concert setting or in a special choir presentation of a baroque

cantata by Bach, Buxtehude, or others. However, this music originally was intended to be sung in a service of worship by the people
in the pews, not the choir in the loft. *The United Methodist Hymnal*
has a fine selection of these chorales and any congregation would
benefit from singing some of them as they are printed. But there
are other ways to adapt these hymns.

The rhythm of congregational hymns during the time of Martin
Luther was quite different from today. It was less regular, what we
might today call "syncopated." It was grouped by phrases of text
rather than continual repetition of three- and four-beat measures.
The tempo was quicker and livelier, with a dancelike quality. *The
Lutheran Hymnal and Book of Worship* contains an optional rhythmic setting of "A Mighty Fortress Is Our God" which is excellent to
demonstrate this authentic rhythmic performance. Though different from our accustomed style, it is quite singable, and the choir
could easily learn it. Here is the opening line of this hymn using the
original rhythmic patterns:

Figure 5

Another way to adapt these chorales for congregational use is to
allow the congregation to sing them in their well-known settings
usually performed in choral concerts. Examples would be "Jesu, Joy

of Man's Desiring" and "Sleepers, Awake." Both of these chorales are frequently presented as organ solos in settings by Bach, with or without the choir. Most people are somewhat familiar with these settings and could, with proper direction and choir leadership, sing the full choral cantata settings which would retain the organ's elaborate accompaniment.

(5) **Pentatonic Hymns in Canon.** Some hymns, especially some of the early American hymns, are written so that the melody line utilizes only the first, second, third, fifth, and sixth notes of the major scale. These are the black notes on the piano beginning on F♯ (F♯, G♯, A♯, C♯, and D♯), or in the key of C, the notes C, D, E, G, and A. Together these five notes are called the pentatonic scale. Because of the nature of the harmony which results when these notes are combined, hymns using the pentatonic scale can be sung as a round or a canon (just like "Row, Row, Row Your Boat"), with or without accompaniment.

"How Firm a Foundation" is the best example. The congregation can be divided into any number of parts from two to sixteen. Depending on the number of divisions, each part can begin singing at almost any point of the melody. The result of combining different groups singing the same melody at different intervals is not at all harmonically dissonant, and it can be an exciting experience for a congregation.

Another variation of this technique is to combine together different pentatonic hymns. One example is to divide the congregation into three parts and have each section sing its own hymn, using "How Firm a Foundation," "Amazing Grace" (in 4/4 rather than 3/4 time), and "God, Who Stretched the Spangled Heavens" or some other text using the familiar tune HOLY MANNA.

One suggestion is that you rehearse this technique with the congregation before it is to be used in the service, perhaps at a congregational dinner, at a Sunday school gathering, or during the time before the service begins. It sounds much more complicated than it really is, and people will quickly catch on. Another suggestion is to have a different leader for each section.

In considering authentic performance practice of hymns, ask yourself if the custom in your congregation is to sing vastly different hymns all in the same style. If so, consider the results. Can exciting and vital congregational singing result from singing "A Mighty Fortress Is Our God," "Standing on the Promises," and "He Touched Me" all in the same style? And should that homogenous style be accompanied by the piano or organ? Should the organist play with or without tremolo? Must volume and tempo be fairly uniform also? Or can the original intended style of the hymn play a role in determining how you will sing the hymn? By recovering something of an authentic performance practice in hymn singing, will the congregation realize a heightened awareness of the text? Will incorporating a variety of styles of hymn singing result in a strengthening and invigorating of our prevailing style?

g. Metrical Singing. You search and search for just the right hymn for a specific need in the service. You finally find it, but you see that the tune is totally unfamiliar to the people. You want to use it the following Sunday and you don't have time to introduce it gradually over a period of weeks. The answer is metrical singing. Count the syllables of each line of text. Most hymns will fall into a recognizable pattern. For instance, "Amazing Grace" is 8686. "Joyful, Joyful, We Adore Thee" is 87878787, or 8787D (D means doubled). "For All the Saints" is 10.10.10 with Alleluias. Most hymnals contain a metrical index which groups hymn tunes into their common metrical pattern. If the new and unfamiliar hymn you've selected for the following Sunday has the same meter as one of these patterns, try singing it to a more familiar tune with the same meter.

Metrical singing can also be used to change the tunes of familiar hymns for the sake of variety. As with authentic performance practice, the effect is often one of the congregation hearing and appreciating the text anew. The method is the same as described above. Hymns with the same meter are often interchangeable. Following is a short list of familiar hymns which could be sung to each other's tunes. There are hundreds of other possibilities.

- "For the Beauty of the Earth" and "Rock of Ages"
- "Love Divine All Loves Excelling" and "Come, Thou Fount of Every Blessing"
- "All Hail the Power of Jesus' Name" and "O for a Thousand Tongues"
- "This Is My Father's World" and "Crown Him with Many Crowns"
- "What a Friend We Have in Jesus" and "Joyful, Joyful, We Adore Thee"
- "For All the Saints" and "When in Our Music God Is Glorified"

This technique, however, is not without its problems. Consider the case of "Amazing Grace" and "Joy to the World." Metrically they are interchangeable, but there are three problems. First, the tunes may be inextricably wed to their respective texts, making this exchange particularly difficult for the congregation. Second, textual accent is a problem. "Amazing Grace" accents the second syllable of "amazing," while "Joy to the World" accents the first word. Exchanging the tunes results in an awkward stressing of the wrong syllable. Third, the repetition of the final phrase of "Joy to the World" does not occur in "Amazing Grace." This requires some prior understanding of what portion of the "Amazing Grace" text will be repeated to fill the additional lines of the "Joy to the World" refrain.

Also consider "Stand Up, Stand Up for Jesus" and "O Sacred Head

Now Wounded." Again they are metrically interchangeable, but stylistically the tune of one is totally unsuited to the text of the other. The quiet intensity of the PASSION CHORALE tune does not support the fervor and militancy of the other's text. Likewise, singing the text of "O Sacred Head" to the tune of "Stand Up, Stand Up for Jesus" might border on the sacrilegious.

But as a means of varying a congregation's hymn singing and incorporating new, unfamiliar texts to familiar and even favorite tunes, metrical singing is a method almost any congregation could use.

Metrical singing also includes the possibility of adapting secular tunes to a sacred text for use in worship. This has been a long-standing practice in Christianity, dating back centuries to the Middle Ages and almost certainly earlier. Secular dance tunes were frequently used in worship during the Renaissance period. Complete musical settings of the Roman Catholic mass often made use of folk songs and other secular tunes in the *cantus firmus* or as a repeated theme. For centuries Christianity has incorporated local traditions, including music, when missionaries and evangelists moved into a new area. Closer to the present day, General William Booth and his Salvation Army went to great lengths to incorporate secular music in its worship, believing that to do so would bring more of the lost and suffering into the faith. The American revival and campmeeting movement spawned hundreds of new hymns and songs, many of them rooted in popular and folk traditions. Even today, we continue to sing hymns in contemporary worship to tunes of secular origin, such as "The Battle Hymn of the Republic." We even sing the national anthem of the United States, "The Star Spangled Banner," to the tune of an early American drinking song. One is not surprised, then, to attend a Sunday evening worship service and be asked to sing the text of Fanny Crosby's "Blessed Assurance, Jesus Is Mine" to the tune of Stephen Foster's "Beautiful

Dreamer," nor should one be surprised to hear a contemporary soloist singing the pop song "Feelings" with the name *Jesus* substituted for the word *feelings,* complete with the "wo-wo-wo's."

The practice of adapting the secular to sacred use has been a continuing controversy since the practice began early in Christian history. But if your congregational singing can be renewed and invigorated through the adaptation of secular tunes to sacred texts in worship, and if it can be done with proper taste, style, and grace, then you should pursue this resource. However, be aware of some of the legal restrictions and obtain the proper permissions beforehand. Only a few short years ago hundreds of United Methodist and other congregations were singing a congregational benediction to the tune of "Edelweiss" from *The Sound of Music,* and were threatened with fines and lawsuits by the owners of the musical copyright.

8. Promote Singing Outside Sunday Morning Worship. Any time church members gather should be a time for singing. Take every opportunity you can to incorporate group singing into whatever purpose people have come together. You can sing at weddings, funerals, and memorial services; church dinners and picnics; Sunday school classes and parties; United Methodist Men, Women, and Youth functions; meetings of church boards, agencies, and committees; children as well as adults will sing on a bus, in a van, or in a car on the way to their destination. If singing comes to be seen as a valuable activity outside of worship, it will take on greater importance within worship.

Encourage church members to purchase a hymnal and use it in their homes. One church was able to purchase new hymnals for its pews by encouraging families and individuals to donate one or more copies to the church as a memorial and at the same time order one for their own home use. Hymnals are an invaluable resource for private and family devotions. Hymns can be used by parents to instruct themselves and their children in our 2000 years of theology and history. As with all other elements of faith, acts within worship are strengthened when practiced as a part of daily living.

Good, strong congregational singing is not an accident. It does not simply happen naturally of its own accord. Good congregational singing is the result of intentional planning on the part of a number of worship participants: pastor, music director, accompanists, choir members, Council on Ministries and Worship Work Area leaders, Staff-Parish Relations Committee members, trustees, Finance Committees, and church architects. Not only does it require planning and implementation, it also requires constant attention, evaluation, experimentation, and encouragement. And through it all our aim should be the same as John Wesley's: "So shall your singing be such as the Lord will approve here, and reward you when he cometh in the clouds of heaven."

4
Hymn Festivals

Hymn festival is the collective title for a number of different types of song services. One type is a service of worship and praise. Another is a service in commemoration of a person, such as a composer or author; of an event, such as the Reformation or the Bicentennial of the United States; or, of a unifying theme or topic, such as British hymns or hymns by women. Yet another type of hymn festival is one designed to explore and make use of the different vocal and instrumental musical resources which may be used in hymn singing.

A hymn festival primarily intended for the purpose of worship can be planned for a weeknight service, a Sunday evening, or even a Sunday morning. One method would be to sing a hymn for each act of worship: call to worship, hymn of praise, confession, Lord's Prayer, hymns as scripture, offertory, and even the sermon can consist of hymns in whole or in part. A worship service of congregational singing can be organized around the season of the year or even the entire liturgical year.

On a larger, more ambitious scale, a hymn festival may include a number of congregations and choirs. The festival may utilize multiple directors and organists. In such a gathering, the service may be organized around a season, an event, a holiday, a commonly used creed or scripture (Apostles' Creed, Nicene Creed, Lord's Prayer, Ten Commandments), or one or more of the great hymn writers (Wesley, Watts, Luther, Crosby, Pratt Green). The service will take on a celebrational and ecumenical nature, cutting across differences of denomination, worship, music style, and theology.

When planned for the local congregation, a hymn festival can be not only a worship experience, but also an opportunity for fellowship and for encouraging, teaching, or rehearsing congregational singing. In such a service the people come together for the single purpose and expectation of singing together. The director can adopt a less formal role, giving suggestions and encouragement for improving singing, giving biographical and historical information about hymns, and using congregational singing as a tool for teaching the people on a range of subjects as diverse as theology or music fundamentals.

Hymn festivals should make extensive use of all the musical resources available for congregational singing. Accompaniments should be varied to include: organ and piano separately and together; other instruments (handbells, brass, strings, winds, percussion, full orchestra); alternate organ harmonizations and instrumental descants; stanzas given over completely to one or more instruments; a capella stanzas; and different accompanists. Congregational singing should be varied to include: responsive and antiphonal singing; stanzas read silently or aloud in unison; congregation in unison and in parts; various performance practices; metrical singing; and various groupings within the congregation (sex, age, location in the sanctuary, denomination). Variety can be introduced through using different vocal forces: soprano descants; choir in unison or parts; choral settings from masterworks; choir in balcony or surrounding the congregation; a cappella choir; and stanzas by a soloist, duet, trio, quartet, or other ensemble. The possibilities for varying congregational singing in hymn festivals are virtually limitless.

Equally limitless are the possibilities for organizing a hymn festival around a unifying theme. Here are only a few suggestions.

Historical Events

Reformation Hymns	Campmeeting and Revival Hymns
Catholic Hymns Since Vatican II	Wartime Hymns

Authors and Composers

The Wesleys   Isaac Watts
Fanny Crosby   Lowell Mason
James Montgomery   Frederick Pratt Green
Fred Kaan   Bach Chorales
Ralph Vaughan Williams   Peter Cutts and Brian Wren
Bill and Gloria Gaither   Martin Luther
Ira Sankey   John Peterson
Charles Gabriel   Frances Havergal
Georgia Harkness   living composers and authors
hymns adapted from poets   female composers and authors
hymns translated into English

The Calendar

any liturgical season   the complete liturgical year
secular holidays and observances
   (New Year's Day, Independence
   Day/Patriotic, Thanksgiving,
   harvest, Labor Day)

Ethnic Hymns

Irish   German
English   North American
Latin American   Black Hymns and Spirituals
Asian   Native American
Third World Hymns   European
Welsh

Year Commemorative

Select a specific year and sing hymn tunes and texts composed and
published or authors and composers born and died at periodic intervals
prior to that year. For example, for the commemorative year 1990, select
hymns from the year 1980, 1965, 1940, 1890, 1840, 1790, 1740, etc.

Scripture Themes

The Psalms   Psalm 23, 150, or others
John 3:16   The Beatitudes
The Lord's Prayer   Scripture Choruses

Theological and Credal Topics

Salvation   The Trinity

Faith, Hope, and Love	The Cross
Christ's Second Coming	The Church
Missions and Evangelism	Prophecy
Apostles' Creed	Social Creed
Nicene Creed	Te Deum

Denominational Hymns

Methodist	Baptist
Presbyterian	Anglican
Roman Catholic	Jewish
Moravian	Lutheran
Salvation Army	Christian Science
Unitarian/Universalist	Restoration Traditions

Numerous examples of hymn festivals, including printed programs, articles, pamphlets, and resources on how to plan, organize, and carry out a festival, are available from The Hymn Society of America, Inc., National Headquarters, Texas Christian University, P.O. Box 30854, Fort Worth, TX 76129.

One of the best reasons for organizing a hymn festival, aside from the practical benefits of strengthening congregational singing, is to introduce the congregation to a new hymnal. Discovering the contents of a new hymnal becomes itself the unifying framework for the festival. The prevailing spirit and excitement of a hymn festival can generate continued enthusiasm as a congregation exchanges its comfortably worn and familiar hymnal with an unknown new one.

5
Getting Started

This chapter is written specifically to offer suggestions and encouragement to pastors and laypersons in churches with small membership, small budgets, and few if any trained musicians. If you are an accomplished musician, the pastor or staff member of a large church with a full music and worship ministry, or part of an active, ongoing church music ministry, then skip this chapter. But if you are just beginning and your resources are modest, if you don't know what to do next, or if you want to try to organize a small volunteer church choir for the purpose of supporting and leading congregational singing, then read on.

Get Help

Talk with the pastor and other lay people in the church who may be interested in getting a choir started. Perhaps four or five persons could meet periodically as a Music Committee. Work with the chairperson of the Worship Work Area as well as the Council On Ministries or the Administrative Council of your church. Arrive at an understanding of what you would like to achieve and explore ways to do it.

Seek help and advice outside your congregation. Each district has a district chairperson for worship and a Council on Ministries. Contact the district office to learn who those persons are and inquire into what resources and help they may be able to provide. Talk with the pastor or music director of a larger church in your area if there is one. You will discover that many people will be eager to help you in your task.

Your annual conference may have a worship committee or discipleship chairperson who could offer resources and suggestions. The Conference Council Director should also be able to assist you, either directly or by putting you in contact with persons who can.

Many agencies and groups, both within and without The United Methodist Church, can offer invaluable assistance. Contact one or more of them. Some of them include: The United Methodist Publishing House; your local Cokesbury bookstores; Discipleship Resources; the Upper Room; the General Board of Discipleship Section on Worship; The Fellowship of United Methodists in Worship, Music and Other Arts; The Hymn Society of America; Choristers Guild; and The American Guild of Organists. (See Appendix.) These groups and agencies make available books, pamphlets, magazines, journals, articles, tapes, records, movies, filmstrips, and other resources all designed for just your purpose of getting a small choir together to support congregational singing. Some of them can even offer personal assistance on the telephone if needed.

Remember that you do not have to do it all by yourself!

Take an Inventory

What is available in your church for accompanying? Do you have a piano and/or an organ? Is the instrument's condition in need of repair? If you need to obtain one, let the need be known to members and friends of the congregation. Perhaps someone has one at home which could be loaned or donated. Is there a larger church in your area which would loan or donate an instrument to you?

What is available in your church for the choir to sing? Is there a music library or file used in the past? If so, is the music usable today or does some or most of it need to be disposed of? As you are just getting started, you may prefer to use the hymnal as the primary source for choir music. It offers much music suitable for choir use, especially for smaller groups or for a choir made up of mostly nonmusician volunteers. Again, don't hesitate to seek assistance from a larger church in your area. Many churches would be willing to loan choral music for your use.

Recruit

If your main objective is to have a choir to lead and encourage congregational singing, then begin looking in your own congregation for singers. Let your purpose be known. Let the people know it is not your intention to sing Bach cantatas or Mendelssohn oratorios or to stage extravagant contemporary musicals. Let them know that congregational singing is a vitally important part of congregational worship. The mere physical presence of a group of people committed to making that aspect of worship more meaningful for themselves and other worshipers will do much to make it so. You are not looking for people who consider themselves musicians or singers. You are looking for people who recognize the importance of hymn singing and who are willing to commit some time and energy each week in preparation.

Recruit from your entire congregation—old, young, middle-aged, men, women, long-time members, and new members. The best choir singers are those who may have had a bit of musical training in their lives. Perhaps they played an instrument for a couple of years in the band. Maybe they once had piano lessons. You might even have a school music teacher or a piano teacher among your people. Seek those persons out. Their past experience and knowledge of music can be renewed and they will become leaders within your choir. One of them might even be willing to take on the role of director or accompanist. And don't neglect the youth. Older children and teenagers can contribute their time and talent just as do adults. An intergenerational choir can be a marvelous experience for the singers and for the congregation, and it says something about your church's commitment to ministering to persons of all ages.

What about Leadership?

As the person getting things started, you might very well take on the role of director, even if you don't have formal musical training. Remember, your goal is to lead and encourage congregational singing, not train a group of professional singers. You can seek help from sources already mentioned. If you are doubtful of your ability to direct a choir, specifically ask for suggestions from another director in your area. He or she can quickly show you the basics of beat patterns, time signatures, phrasing, note reading, and other music fundamentals. But some of these things will come naturally to you as you gain on-the-job experience. You will discover that your expertise and your self-confidence will grow with experience. The most important requirement is to use your ears to listen to the group. You will hear differences in pitch, pronunciation, and tone quality. You don't have to be a singing instructor to hear these and then tell the choir about them. They will be eager to accept your direction and make the needed corrections. They will want to do the best possible job of being worship leaders.

Once someone is recruited to serve as director, encourage that person to take advantage of any workshops or conferences sponsored in your district, conference, or elsewhere. Dozens of these are available each year for all aspects of worship and church music, including leading a small, volunteer church choir.

Plan

Work with the pastor and lay leadership involved in worship. If possible, learn what seasonal events will be observed in the coming weeks. Will the pastor preach a special series for Lent? What will be the sermon subjects and scripture texts? Have the hymns been selected? Can you help in the selection of hymns for worship? When you know the answers to these questions, the choir can then rehearse music further ahead than for just the coming Sunday.

Plan your rehearsal time. Allot time for rehearsing the hymns for the coming and for future Sundays. Remember that leading congregational singing should be your primary task, and then spend sufficient time rehearsing the hymns so that the singers are fully prepared to lead singing. If the choir presents music in worship other than hymns, know ahead of the rehearsal how much time you plan to spend practicing each number. Will you learn responses and service music? Each rehearsal should include a time for devotion. This may be as unstructured as an opening or closing prayer. Perhaps choir members can take turns leading a prayer. You can include a short scripture reading or read a short meditation. Each rehearsal should include time for fellowship. Many choirs have a coffee pot, and the members take turns bringing refreshments. This time for fellowship is a time to build relationships and cement friendships. Other opportunities for fellowship throughout the year may include attending a musical production or concert or having a choir potluck supper, a picnic, a skating party, a swimming party, a winter ski trip, or any number of activities. Any one or more of these will build up the spirit and commitment of your choir.

Evaluate

Once you have begun and the choir is singing, follow up with evaluation. This can take place simply by your considering how things are going and ways to improve. Or it may include a more formal process of meeting with the pastor, the Worship Committee, the Council on Ministries, or even the entire choir. Openly discuss what is needed to make the choir leadership more effective. Discuss options and possibilities. Give praise and thanks where they are due. Your goal is a worthy one. Be deliberate and intentional about how you work to achieve it.

Appendix
Worship Resources

The American Guild of Organists, 815 2nd Ave., New York, NY 10017; (212) 687-9188

Choristers Guild, 2834 W. Kingsley Blvd., Garland, TX 75041; (214) 271-1521

Discipleship Resources, Box 189, Nashville, TN 37202; (615) 340-7284

The Fellowship of United Methodists in Worship, Music, and Other Arts, P.O. Box 54367, Atlanta, GA 30308; (405) 577-7914

The Hymn Society of America, Box 30854, Texas Christian University, Fort Worth, TX 76127; (817) 921-7608

Section on Worship, General Board of Discipleship, P.O. Box 840, Nashville, TN 37202; (615) 340-7070

The United Methodist Publishing House, 201 8th Avenue South, Nashville, TN 37203; 749-6000

The Upper Room, 1908 Grand Ave., P.O. Box 189, Nashville, TN 37202-9229; (615) 340-7284